Camden Town Advanced

YOUNG PEOPLE
A guide to text analysis

Erarbeitet von

Stephanie Claussen
Pamela Hanus
Christoph Reuter
Mirja Schnoor
Sylvia Wauer

Fachliche Beratung

Tanja Golla

Diesterweg

Westermann Schroedel Diesterweg Schöningh Winklers GmbH, Braunschweig
www.diesterweg.de

Druck A^{3} / Jahr 2013
Alle Drucke der Serie A sind im Unterricht parallel verwendbar.

Redaktion: Christoph Golla, Demet Kömür und Daniel Shatwell
Layout: Sandra Grünberg
Illustrationen: Oliver Fuchs, Berlin
Umschlaggestaltung: blum DESIGN & KOMMUNIKATION, Hamburg
Gestaltung und Satz: RSRDesign Reckels & Schneider-Reckels, Wiesbaden
Druck und Bindung: Westermann Druck GmbH, Zwickau

ISBN 978-3-425-**06651**-6

Contents

Contents

Contents

1

Family relationships

Language support

Judging from the photo, the family seems ...
Considering their facial expressions, they may ...
If you look at their body language, you get the impression that ...

Getting started

A1 Describe the families in the photos.

A2 Speculate what the photos reveal about the family relationships.

A3 Look at the pictogram of a nuclear family. Choose two of the types of family from the box. Visualize these by creating pictograms for them.

- blended family
- step family
- same-sex couples with children
- single-parent family
- nuclear family
- extended family

A4 Discuss what families are for and what positive and negative relationships exist between family members. Visualize your ideas in a graphic organizer.

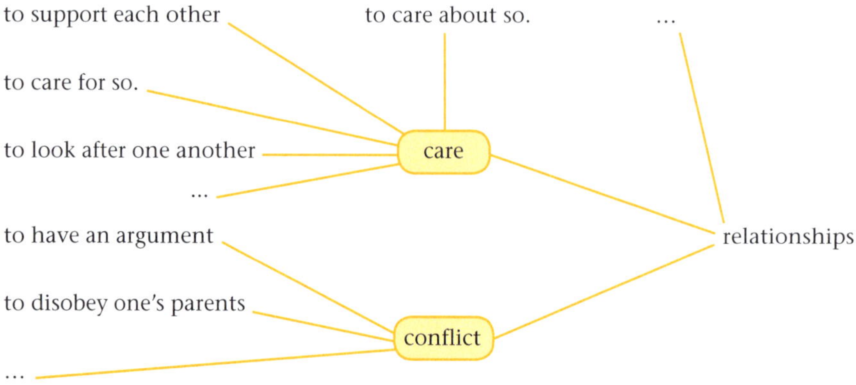

A5 a) Listen to the song "Family Portrait" by Pink. What's your immediate reaction to the song?

b) Listen again and say what the song is about in two to three sentences.

c) Describe the hopes and fears expressed in the song.

DVD

Language support

The song deals with …

The lyrics reveal that …

A6 a) Compare the family relationships described in the song to how you see the families in the photos.

b) Find or describe a photo that would go with Pink's song and explain your choice.

Family portrait

Momma please stop cryin', I can't stand the sound
Your pain is painful and it's tearin' me down
I hear glasses breakin' as I sit up in my bed
I told Dad you didn't mean those nasty things you said

You fight about money, 'bout me and my brother
And this I come home to, this is my shelter
It ain't easy growin' up in World War III
Never knowin' what love could be, you'll see
I don't want love to destroy me like it has done my family

Chorus
Can we work it out? Can we be a family?
I promise I'll be better, Mommy I'll do anything
Can we work it out? Can we be a family?
I promise I'll be better, Daddy please don't leave

Daddy please stop yellin', I can't stand the sound
Make Mama stop cryin', cuz I need you around
My mama she loves you, no matter what she says it's true
I know that she hurts you, but remember I love you, too

I ran away today, ran from the noise, ran away
Don't wanna go back to that place, but don't have no choice, no way
It ain't easy growin' up in World War III
Never knowin' what love could be, well I've seen
I don't want love to destroy me like it did my family

Chorus

In our family portrait, we look pretty happy
Let's play pretend, let's act like it comes naturally
I don't wanna have to split the holidays
I don't want two addresses
I don't want a step-brother anyways
And I don't want my mom to have to change her last name

In our family portrait we look pretty happy
We look pretty normal, let's go back to that
In our family portrait we look pretty happy
Let's play pretend, act like it goes naturally

[…]

Daddy don't leave
Turn around please
Remember that the night you left you took my shining star?
Daddy don't leave
Don't leave us here alone

Mom will be nicer
I'll be so much better, I'll tell my brother
Oh, I won't spill the milk at dinner
I'll be so much better, I'll do everything right
I'll be your little girl forever
I'll go to sleep at night

Practice section

Pre-reading

B1 You are going to read a short story by Dallas Woodburn. Its title is "Red". What do you associate with this colour?

B2 Read the first part of the story (ll.1–12).
a) Describe Grace's reaction to spilling the nail polish.

b) Comment on her reaction.

Grace knocked the nail polish off her bedside table and onto the carpet and that was The End. She crouched there, as if paralyzed, watching the Maybelline "Vixen Red" soak into the white Burbur[1], the teardrop-shaped stain[2] slowly growing bigger and bigger, like blood seeping[3] into a Band-Aid.

Grace sat there, rocking[4] on her heels, watching and waiting. Waiting and watching. For what, she didn't exactly know. When the teardrop stopped growing, she got up and went to the kitchen to get some paper towels.

[1] **Burbur** = a kind of carpet
[2] **stain** = Fleck
[3] **to seep** = sickern
[4] **to rock** = to swing backwards and forwards

Comprehension: Summary writing

Summary: Identifying the theme/Introductory sentence

B3 Read the rest of the story.

The rain spattered softly against the car windows. Grace watched the windshield wipers dance, back and forth, forth and back, like her piano teacher's metronome. She sat with her knees hugged up against her chin, trying to minimize the contact of her skin with the cold vinyl[5]. "Mom," she said. "It's raining cats and frogs."

"You mean cats and *dogs*," her mother corrected, never taking her eyes off the road. It was still raining "cats and frogs" when they arrived at the park. Grace stared out the car window and imagined they were inside a giant aquarium, except filled with birds instead of fish.

Her mother turned around and smiled at Grace in the backseat. "What a perfect day," she said, "to fly a kite!" Grace could tell she wasn't joking. Her mother never joked about important matters.

Part of Grace wanted to stay in the car, but the other part of her won out[6]. She pulled the strings on her sweatshirt hood so tight her face was scrunched[7] and there was only a keyhole of an opening where the rain could get in. Then she tied the strings in a bow[8]- double-knotted, the way Grampa had taught her so it wouldn't come undone[9].

Grace tightly held her mother's hand as they trudged[10] together up the rain-slickened hill that overlooked the playground. Grace had never been to the park in the rain. It was deserted. Like a magic kingdom that belonged only to Grace and her mother. Just the two of them, and of course some fish disguised as birds. "We've always got each other, Hon," her mom said whenever Grace asked about her daddy. "Us girls gotta stick together. Just you and me, that's all we need."

That's all we need. Just you and me. Grace squeezed her mother's hand.

They were at the top of the hill now, and Grace peeked out her keyhole through the drizzle at the slide and the swingset[11], then at the picnic tables and the scattered trees, and finally at their blue Volvo parked alongside the curb. Her mother stood a few feet away, face turned skyward, eyes squinting[12] against the driving

[5] **vinyl** = tough, shiny plastic material
[6] **to win out** = sich durchsetzen
[7] **to scrunch** = to press into a smaller shape
[8] **bow** = the kind of knot you tie when you tie shoe-laces
[9] **undone** = not tied
[10] **to trudge** = to walk with slow, heavy steps
[11] **swingset** = a group of seats hanging from chains that move backwards and forwards
[12] **to squint** = to close your eyes slightly and try to see sth.

BBs[13] of water, hair streaming long and wet down her back. Grace's clothes had grown heavy and cumbersome. All the tiny raindrops had banded together. It reminded Grace of one of her Grampa's favorite sayings.

"Take little steps, baby steps," he told Grace whenever she was on the brink of[14] giving up. "Baby steps have a way of adding up to a lot of big steps."

"So do raindrops," Grace thought now, wriggling inside her soggy *Hello Kitty* sweatshirt. "Little raindrops have a way of adding up to big buckets." She wanted to take her sweatshirt off but couldn't get Grampa's double-knotted bow undone. Water ran off the tip of her nose and she stuck out her tongue and caught a drop. She was surprised at how warm it tasted.

Grace's mother held the kite with hopeful outstretched hands. She peered up into the leaden sky as if challenging it, or maybe begging. The kite was small and diamond-shaped and painted with rainbows, which Grace's mother said was "highly ironic." Grace smiled appreciatively even though she didn't know what "ironic" meant. She knew this though: she loved kites and she loved rainbows. And, above all, she loved her mother.

The kite had a hard time getting airborne. "Mom, maybe we should go," Grace said, holding the end of the kite string and shivering slightly, but her mother didn't hear. Grace's mother continued to squint into the drizzle, determined and desperate, holding the kite above her head, quietly beseeching[15] the wind to take the tiny rainbow in its arms and raise it high. Grace knew you shouldn't fly kites in the rain. Her mother knew this too, and yet there she stood, trying anyway. *Just you and me, Hon*[16]. Years later, this was what Grace most vividly remembered when she thought of her mother: eyes squinted toward the heavens, a double-knot bow that just wouldn't come undone, and a tiny rainbow struggling against the rain to fly.

* * *

The chemotherapy started the very next week.

The second time, Grace went with her mother into The Little White Room with the hospital smell and space-age machinery. It reminded Grace of the aliens she had seen once, when her Uncle Bill let her stay up late and watch a movie with The Big Kids. Grace was scared of The Little White Room but she went in anyway. She sat beside the bed and watched the medicine *drip ... drip ... drip* out of the IV bag[17], down a clear tube, and into her mother's arm, slowly trickling inside her, becoming a part of her, like blood or bone.

Drip ... drip ... drip It reminded Grace of rain dripping off the leaves of the eucalyptus trees at the park, the day she and her mother flew the rainbow kite. Grace remembered the way her mother shrieked with excitement when the wind finally swept the kite up into its arms. Grace's heart leapt with the thrill of the kite tugging on the string. She forgot about her soggy sweatshirt and stubborn double-knot bow. She and her mother stood side-by-side, *just you and me, Hon,* watching the rainbow dance in the gray misty rain.

"Hey Mom," Grace said now, eyes still transfixed[18] on the IV bag. "It's like the rain."

"That's nice, Honey." But Grace could tell her mother wasn't really listening. She didn't watch the *drip ... drip ... drip*. Instead, she looked at Grace and asked her questions about kindergarten and play-dates and Grandma and Grampa. She sounded tired.

As the treatments continued, Grace sometimes brought along pictures she drew in art class. This always made her mother smile, except for the picture of the rainbow kite and the rain. That one made her mother cry.

One day when Grace came to The Little White Room she brought a bottle of her mother's nail polish and they painted each other's toenails. Grace was careful as could be, but she still got polish on the skin around her mother's nails. She wasn't very good at "coloring inside the lines," but her mother said that was okay. The nail polish was red; deep red; "Vixen Red." It was her mother's favorite color. She said it made her feel alive. After all, you couldn't be dying if you had bright red toenails. It just didn't fit the picture.

Grace believed her. *We've always got each other, Hon. Just you and me.* She coated[19] her mother's toenails with thick layers of red, as if somehow chip-free[20] nails could create miracles.

[13] **BBs** = bullet balls = Schrotkugeln
[14] **to be on the brink of doing sth.** = to be about to do sth.
[15] **to beseech** = to ask for sth. very urgently and sincerely
[16] **Hon** = short for "honey", synonym is "darling"
[17] **IV bag** = intravenous bag
[18] **transfixed** = to be so shocked about sth. that you don't move
[19] **coat of paint** = a layer of paint which has been put on a surface
[20] **chip-free** = not having any marks or cracks

And then her mother died, and Grace's eyes were Vixen Red for weeks, and she didn't believe in miracles anymore.

* * *

Grace kept the $3.49 bottle of Vixen Red polish in her bureau[20] drawer buried underneath her underwear, where nobody would find it. She kept some of her mother's other things – a lock of auburn hair, a lavender silk scarf, a book of Walt Whitman poems – in the drawer of her bedside table. But the nail polish was Grace's secret treasure. Sometimes she would slip it out and painstakingly[21] paint a single fingernail red with the same tiny brush that had traced her mother's nails nearly a decade ago. Now she stayed "inside the lines," carefully painting only one coat, using as little polish as possible, because this was a magical red, her mother's red, and she couldn't go out and buy more when she ran out. She doubted they even made Vixen Red anymore.

Grace would sit there on her bedroom floor, sneaking glances at the splash of vibrant color alive against the white of her skin, stroking the single red nail with her thumb, strangely comforted yet upset with herself at the same time.

Now, Grace watched the pool of Vixen Red soak through the layers of paper towels. The tiny bottle, nearly empty, was propped upright on the bedside table.

She looked out the window. It was raining "cats and frogs." Tears spilled from her eyes and *drip … drip … dripped* down her cheeks, but Grace felt a smile cracking her face. She crawled across the floor and rummaged around in the back of her closet.

Grace sat there for a moment, looking at it, running her hand across the light plastic surface. With Vixen Red-stained fingers, she carefully wiped off a thin film of dust. *Baby steps,* she thought, taking a deep breath. *Baby steps.*

She slipped out the front door and into the rain, hugging the faded rainbow tightly to her chest. *Baby steps. Baby steps.* Grace opened her mouth wide and caught a water droplet on her tongue.

"What a perfect day," she thought, smiling as she squinted into the falling raindrops, "to fly a kite."

[20] **bureau** = a writing desk with small shelves and drawers
[21] **painstakingly** = very carefully

B4 a) Identifying the theme: from the sentences below, choose the one that sums up best what the story is about.
Keep in mind that the sentence should not just give a brief overview of the action, but express the main theme or conflict of the text.

> The short story "Red" by Dallas Woodburn, published in 2005, deals with …
>
> 1. … Grace's life as a young child when her mother was still alive and her life as a teenager.
> 2. … how shocked she is about spilling her mother's nail polish.
> 3. … how Grace remembers her mother and feels about her.
> 4. … how Grace as a young adult is unable to overcome the grief over the death of her mother when she was a small child.

b) Discuss your choices in class.

c) Look at the introductory sentences.
What other information must you include in addition to the theme?

Summary: Outlining the structure

B5 When you are writing the summary of a text, imagine the summary is for someone who has not read the text and needs to know the essence of what the text is about. In order to identify the main elements of a story and be able to present them more clearly, it helps to subdivide a story into meaningful parts and use those parts as a basis for the summary. A change of the setting, i. e. the time and place of action, the characters and topic can signal the beginning of a new section.

Skills
How to write a summary p. 82

a) Outline the structure of the story.

b) Identify where the remaining parts start and end and add the line numbers. Subdivide longer parts into meaningful units where necessary. Which of the criteria mentioned above can be used to subdivide the story?

c) Make notes for each part to sum up the most important points.

ll. 1-xx	*Grace: nail polish knocked over* *nail polish ⟶ dead mother* *⟶ shock*
ll. xy-zz	*…*

B6 Use your results from B4 and B5 to write a summary of "Red".

Skills
How to write a summary p. 82

Checklist

- ✓ Use the present tense.
- ✓ Present events in a chronological order.
- ✓ Don't quote from the text. Use your own words.
- ✓ Don't start analyzing the text.
- ✓ Don't give your personal opinion.
- ✓ Use connectives to link your sentences.

Analysis

Analyzing the narrative perspective

B7 The narrative perspective is used to describe the point of view from which the story is viewed. The narrator of a story can influence the readers by the way he/she tells the story, so it is important to identify the narrator.

a) Look at text A – a passage from "Red". Then compare it with the altered versions B and C. Point out the differences and their effect on the reader.

A Grace sat there, rocking on her heels, watching and waiting. Waiting and watching. For what, she didn't exactly know. When the teardrop stopped growing, she got up and went to the kitchen to get some paper towels.

B I sat there, watching and waiting. Waiting and watching. I did not know exactly for what I was waiting, maybe it had to do with the fact that the nail polish had reminded me of my mother and her death. When I felt a little better, I got up and went to the kitchen to get a paper towel.

C Grace sat there, watching and waiting. Waiting and watching. For what exactly, she did not know. She hadn't been feeling well these past few days, and now knocking over the nail polish was just the right thing to make her cry again.
Meanwhile, her best friend Amy was sitting in her bedroom, thinking about Grace. Grace had seemed very distracted lately, so Amy was worried. She wished Grace would call her to talk about the things that were troubling her.
Over in her apartment, Grace waited for the teardrops to stop growing, and then she got up and went to the kitchen to get some paper towels.
Sadly, calling Amy never occurred to her.

Info: Perspective

When you want to identify the perspective, there are three main types you have to know:

1. The *first person* narrator
The person who tells the story is also a character in the text – this can be the protagonist, but also a character of minor importance. He/She tells you what he/she knows, how he/she feels and what he/she experiences. The reader can easily identify with a first person narrator, but because this narrator mentions only what he/she knows or wants to mention, the information can be unreliable or subjective.

2. The *third person* omniscient narration
The story is told from the outside, not by a character in the story itself. The narrator knows everything about the characters (thoughts, emotions, etc.) and the plot, and as a result the reader is informed about everything and often knows more than the characters in the story. The third person omniscient narrator also comments on the story and the characters.

3. The *third person* limited narration
The story is told from the outside, but as if seen through the eyes of one of the characters. Note that this character is not the narrator, though. The reader only perceives and knows the same things as the character that is the focus of the narration.

Language support
The narration provides an insight into ...
In this story, you can identify a ...
The narration concentrates on ...
The point of view is restricted to ...

b) Identify the type of narration used in "Red" and write one paragraph explaining its effects on the reader. Use your ideas from a).

Analyzing the language – stylistic devices

B8 There are many aspects one can look at when analyzing the language of a text – the register (e.g. slang, formal English), the choice of words or the style.
For "Red", it is useful to focus on some stylistic devices.
Stylistic devices are used to underline the message of a story, to create a certain atmosphere or to highlight important aspects.
Several stylistic devices are prominent in the short story "Red":

Tip
Never look at the language as an isolated part of a story – you have to combine language and content in your text analysis!

Info: Stylistic devices

Simile = a comparison of two ideas, often linked by "as" or "like"
Example: *"Like a magic kingdom that belonged only to Grace and her mother."* (ll. 43–44)

Metaphor = two ideas that are normally not linked are compared in a metaphor without using "as" or "like"
Example: *"Her mother stood a few feet away, face turned skyward, eyes squinting against the driving BBs of water [...]"* (ll. 57–59)

Symbol = an image that does not only stand for itself but also signifies a more abstract concept or idea
Example: *"Baby steps have a way of adding up to a lot of big steps."* (ll. 66–67)

Repetition = words or phrases that are used more than once in a text, catching the reader's attention
Example: *"She knew this though: she loved kites and she loved rainbows. And, above all, she loved her mother."* (ll. 84–86)

a) Get together in small groups. There should be at least one group for each topic.
Each group should make a grid like this:

stylistic device/quote	*meaning*	*effect*

Group 1
Fill in your grid with examples of similes and metaphors from "Red".

Group 2
Fill in your grid with examples of symbolism from "Red".

Group 3
Fill in your grid with examples of repetitions from "Red".

b) Form new groups – in each group, there must be at least one "expert" for every stylistic device.
Inform the others in your group about your results. Take notes when they present their results, too.

Skills
How to write a text analysis p. 83

B9 Analyze the following extract from the short story. The checklist below will help you.

Grace tightly held her mother's hand as they trudged together up the rain-slickened hill that overlooked the playground. Grace had never been to the park in the rain. It was deserted. Like a magic kingdom that belonged only to Grace and her mother. Just the two of them, and of course some fish disguised as birds. "We've always got each other, Hon," her mom said whenever Grace asked about her daddy. "Us girls gotta stick together. Just you and me, that's all we need."

That's all we need. Just you and me. Grace squeezed her mother's hand.

They were at the top of the hill now, and Grace peeked out her keyhole through the drizzle at the slide and the swingset, then at the picnic tables and the scattered trees, and finally at their blue Volvo parked alongside the curb. Her mother stood a few feet away, face turned skyward, eyes squinting against the driving BBs of water, hair streaming long and wet down her back. Grace's clothes had grown heavy and cumbersome. All the tiny raindrops had banded together. It reminded Grace of one of her Grampa's favorite sayings.

"Take little steps, baby steps," he told Grace whenever she was on the brink of giving up. "Baby steps have a way of adding up to a lot of big steps."

"So do raindrops," Grace thought now, wriggling inside her soggy Hello Kitty sweatshirt. "Little raindrops have a way of adding up to big buckets." She wanted to take her sweatshirt off but couldn't get Grampa's double-knotted bow undone. Water ran off the tip of her nose and she stuck out her tongue and caught a drop. She was surprised at how warm it tasted.

Grace's mother held the kite with hopeful outstretched hands. She peered up into the leaden sky as if challenging it, or maybe begging. The kite was small and diamond-shaped and painted with rainbows, which Grace's mother said was "highly ironic." Grace smiled appreciatively even though she didn't know what "ironic" meant. She knew this though: she loved kites and she loved rainbows. And, above all, she loved her mother.

Checklist

Make sure that you include both language and content:

- ✓ What is being said? (content)
- ✓ How is it being said? (narrative perspective, language)
- ✓ Explain the significance of your results: What do they mean in the context of the story? Do not just list stylistic devices!
- ✓ Describe the effect of the stylistic devices on the reader.

Conclusion

Language support
As pointed out in the analysis …
All in all …
In conclusion, one can say …
… is often shown in the story by …

B10 At the end of your text analysis, you write a paragraph that summarizes your most important results. This is your conclusion.
Check through the results of your analysis and write a conclusion.

Skills
How to structure a text p. 98–100

Comment

Skills
How to write a comment
p. 84–85

After the analysis of a story you will often be asked to comment on a certain problem or aspect from it. A comment is a well-structured text (introduction, first line of argument, second line of argument, conclusion) that should present your opinion as persuasively as possible. In order to achieve that, you have to follow certain steps.

Skills
How to improve your text
p. 94–95

B11 Discuss to what extent Grace has overcome the loss of her mother at the end of the story. Use what you have found out about Grace and her life to collect arguments.

Follow these steps to plan and write your comment:

1. Brainstorming: Know what your line of argument is before you start writing. To do this prewrite or brainstorm your ideas on paper.

2. Outline: Note down your opinion before you start writing the comment. You will have to support it with evidence, so you should collect arguments for and against your opinion.

3. Introduction: The first sentence should be an interesting introduction that presents the problem your comment will discuss.
This could be

- an interesting example.
- a reference to a current discussion.
- a suitable quotation from the text.
- …

4. First line of argument: Look at the problem from one viewpoint (e.g. the viewpoint of those in favour, the arguments for an opinion). Write at least three paragraphs that support your opinion. Because you are commenting on a short story, you can use quotes from the text that support your argument.

5. Second line of argument: Then consider the problem from another viewpoint (e.g. the viewpoint of those against, the arguments against a particular opinion). Address any counter-arguments in the main body of your argument as well.

6. Personal conclusion: End your comment/argument with a paragraph that sums up the evidence presented. Here you say which side or perspective makes more sense to you. Then you should restate your opinion because you have shown how you arrived at that opinion.

Note:
Instead of first discussing arguments in favour and then arguments against, you may also contrast each argument for with an argument against the issue right away.
It is not important to consider every argument there is. Concentrate on the three most important aspects and discuss those in detail.

Language support: commenting		
Introduction	Lines of argument	Conclusion
• The short story (text, novel …) raises the question of/introduces the problem of … • The short story illuminates/ illustrates the problem of … • The short story raises the question if …	• On the one hand …, on the other hand … • In contrast to A, … • Considering the fact that … • Another important fact/ point is that … • Some might argue that …, but … • You have to take into consideration that …	• All in all, … • To sum up, I think … • I have come to the conclusion that … • Personally, … • Looking at the two sides, I have to say … • My final conclusion is that …

Getting to the point

Pre-reading

C1 Read the extract from the short story "Ashes" by Susan Beth Pfeffer and describe the atmosphere. Explain how you have come to your conclusions by referring to the text.

> [...] The diner might have been brand new, but already it had a shabby run-down quality that made it fit right in with the neighborhood. It was two-thirds empty when we got there, and we had our choice of booths. Dad took one that faced the door and sat in the seat where he could check who was coming in. He hadn't done that with me in a long time, and my stomach hurt in an old familiar way. [...]

Comprehension

C2 Summarize the main points of the short story. Pay special attention to changes in location, the characters and the topics addressed in order to divide the text up.

Skills
How to write a summary p. 82

That winter, it felt like every time I saw my father, the sun cast off just a little more warmth than it had the day before. I don't remember a gray day when I saw him. Once it had snowed the night before, and getting to his apartment took longer than normal, as the buses inched[1] their ways past snow-banks and awkwardly parked cars. But the sun made everything glisten[2], and the snow still had a pure look to it, which I knew would be gone by the following morning.

I saw him Tuesdays. I'd been seeing him Tuesdays for almost two years at that point. Before then, it had been Tuesdays and alternate weekends, but as my life got busier, weekends got harder, and Dad didn't complain when we fell instead into a Tuesday-evening ritual. Mom, who was still working on completing her degree, took Tuesday and Thursday evening classes, so I'd go straight to Dad's from school, wait for him to show[3], and then we'd have supper[4] together and talk. It helped that he didn't live a hundred miles away. Just the other end of town, a two-bus-trip ride.

Dad drove me home Tuesday nights, and the moon always shone as brightly as the sun had and the winter stars looked joyful and beckoning[5]. When I was little, Dad used to promise me the stars for a necklace, but like most of his promises, that one never quite happened.

"I'm a dreamer," he said to me more than once, which really wasn't all that different from what Mom said. "He's an irresponsible bum[6]" was her way of wording it. I knew he was both, but I also knew that winter that the sun and the moon dreamed with him.

Sometimes when I haven't seen Dad for a few days, on a Saturday or a Sunday, I'll try to figure out why Mom ever married him. She's the most practical person I know, always putting aside for a rainy day[7]. With Mom, there are a lot of rainy days and she takes a grim sort of pleasure in being ready for them. The flashlight with working batteries for a blackout. The extra quarters when the laundry isn't quite dry. The gift-wrapped bottle of wine for the unexpected and undesired Christmas guest. Her pocketbook overflows with tissues and tampons for anyone who might need them.

Dad gets by[8] on a grin and a willingness to help. He's always there if you need him. Well, not always. He's unexpectedly there, like a warm day in January.

[1] **to inch** = to move very slowly
[2] **to glisten** = to shine as if wet
[3] **to show** = *here:* to arrive at a place where people are expecting you
[4] **supper** = last main meal of the day
[5] **beckoning** = *here:* very attractive
[6] **bum** = *(US) here:* a lazy person
[7] **to put sth. aside for a rainy day** = to save sth. for a time when you may need it
[8] **to get by** = to survive

[…]

"All I can give you is dreams, Ashes," he said to me once. "But one good dream is worth a thousand flashlight batteries."

Ashes. I can still hear the fight. It was just a couple of months before the final breakup. I was in bed, allegedly[9] asleep, when they went at it.

"Her name is Ashleigh!" Mom shouted. "A name you insisted on. So why do you call her 'Ashes'?"

"That's just my nickname for her," Dad replied. He was always harder to hear when they fought. The angrier Mom got, the lower his voice dropped. For some reason, that made her shout even louder.

"But ashes are cold, gray, dead things," Mom yelled. "You're calling your daughter something dead!"

"It's just a nickname," Dad repeated, a little quieter.

"You call her that just to annoy me!" Mom yelled, but Dad's reply was so soft, I could no longer hear him.

A couple of days later, when Dad forgot to pick me up at school, or didn't have the money for the class trip, or got all his favorite kinds of Chinese[10] and none of Mom's and mine, I thought maybe Mom was right, and Dad did call me Ashes just to annoy her.

[…]

It was toward the end of February that winter, and the sun was shining and the air was crisp[11] and clean. I sat waiting for Dad, who I knew would show up eventually[12]. I probably did my homework, or maybe I looked out the window for his car to show. The room he was renting didn't have a TV. Maybe there was a library book to read. Maybe I folded his laundry.

When he got in, he was full of smiles and kisses and I no longer resented[13] the waiting, if I had resented it at all.

[…]

I had, seven days before. But I smiled at Dad, who always seemed to discover the weather each time we visited.

"You look radiant[14]," he said. "You get more and more beautiful. Turn around. Let me admire every single inch."

So I turned around. I was wearing jeans and a bulky[15] brown sweater Mom had given me for Christmas.

"You could be a model," Dad said. "Have you thought about that, Ashes. Modeling? Some of those supermodels make a fortune."

"Dad," I said. "I could never be a supermodel."

"Don't sell yourself short[16]," he replied. "I've read interviews where they say they never thought they were pretty. Not in high school. Just tall and skinny. And you don't have to worry about being tall or skinny."

"I know, Dad," I said. "Which is why I'll never be a supermodel."

He looked at me and then he grinned. "All right," he said. "You're too smart for that kind of work anyway. Be a photographer instead, or a dress designer. You have flair, Ashes. Style. You do something like that, you're sure to make your mark[17]."

Last week he'd told me to be an astronaut. The week before that, the CEO[18] of a Fortune 500[19] corporation. And the week before that, he'd been stunned by my spirituality.

"Oh, Ashes," he said, taking off his winter coat and dropping it on the sofa bed. "I wish I deserved you."

"I wouldn't have any other dad," I told him. "My friends' fathers, they just tell my friends to study more. They never tell them they have flair or style."

"Maybe they don't," Dad said. "You're the special one, Ashes. You're the one-in-a-million girl."

[…]

"One in a million," he said. "And don't let anyone ever tell you otherwise, Ashes. They will, you know. They'll try to tear you down. They'll laugh at your dreams. Even your mother – and she's a saint to have put up with me all those years – even she will discourage you from being all you can be.
I hate to speak against her, but she's not a dreamer, Ashes. She's the most level-headed[20] woman I know. As straight as a yardstick[21]. But

[9] **allegedly** = *here:* as some people believe
[10] **Chinese** = *here:* Chinese takeaway meal
[11] **crisp** = *here:* cold and dry
[12] **eventually** = zum Schluss
[13] **to resent** = to feel unhappy because you think you have not been treated fairly
[14] **radiant** = *here:* extremely happy
[15] **bulky** = big and thick
[16] **to sell yourself short** = to describe yourself as less impressive than you really are
[17] **to make your mark** = to do sth. so that people remember/notice you
[18] **CEO** = Chief Executive Officer = the most senior manager in a company
[19] **Fortune 500** = the 500 largest companies in the US
[20] **level-headed** = behaving in a calm and sensible way
[21] **yardstick** = a stick that is 1 yard (91.4 cm) long and used for measuring things

I was the only dream she ever believed in and once I failed her, she never let herself dream again."

"Mom's all right," I said.

"She certainly is," Dad said. "She's a fine woman."

We were both silent as we pondered[22] Mom. Then Dad laughed. "She'd never let you go hungry," he said. "What do you want for supper, Ashes? I can offer you pizza, Chinese, or fast."

"Anything," I said.

"No, no," he said, and he clapped his hands. "I remember. There's a new diner, opened right around the block. Let's treat ourselves, Ashes, and go out on the town."

"Can you afford it?" I asked, after doing the mental arithmetic[23] of diner versus pizza.

"For a special date with my daughter?" he replied. "Of course I can afford it. Besides, I have something to celebrate."

"What?" I asked.

"I have a chance at something really big," he said." All I need to do is put together a little financing, and I'll be set for life[24]."

"For life?" I said, and I must have sounded like Mom because he stopped smiling.

"All right, not for life," he said. "But it'll be the start of something really big, Ashes. I can feel it. Just a couple hundred bucks, and then all the pieces will fall into place."

I had no idea where Dad thought he could get two hundred dollars. But he looked so happy I had to smile, too.

"Then diner it is," I said, and I got my coat. Dad picked his up from the sofa and put it back on. "Rice pudding[25] for dessert," he said as we walked out the door. "You can always tell the quality of a diner by its rice pudding."

The diner might have been brand new, but already it had a shabby run-down quality that made it fit right in with the neighborhood. It was two-thirds empty when we got there, and we had our choice of booths[26]. Dad took one that faced the door, and sat in the seat where he could check who was coming in. He hadn't done that with me in a long time, and my stomach hurt in an old familiar way.

"Waiting for someone?" I asked him. I stared at the menu, so I wouldn't have to look at him not looking at me.

"Of course not," he said. "Not when I'm with you. Take your pick[27], Ashes. Hamburger, triple-decker, chicken salad platter. Whatever you want."

I ordered the burger and fries, hoping that by the time it came I'd feel like eating. Dad took a quick look at the menu, closed it, and ordered coffee.

"You'll share my fries," I said to him.

He nodded as though we'd just completed a difficult negotiation. "I'll even eat your pickle[28]," he said. But then he looked back at the door.

"What is it?" I asked him.

"It's nothing," he said. "Oh hell, Ashes, you can always see right through me."

He was the one who'd been looking right through me toward the door, but I didn't say anything.

"That money," he said. "The two hundred dollars?"

I nodded.

"Well, it isn't so much for a deal as to help pay off[29] one I already made," Dad said. "But I've got to tell you, honey[30], once that money is paid, I'm on my way to easy street[31]. Just a little setback[32]. But you know how those guys are. They get itchy[33] when you owe them money. And it's not always comfortable to be where they can scratch you."

"You owe them two hundred dollars?" I asked, trying to keep the panic out of my voice.

"Give or take[34]," Dad said. "But don't worry about it, honey. I'll work it out. I always do."

My burger and fries came then. Dad took a long sip of his coffee, while I poured ketchup on my plate and twirled[35] a fry in it. "Can I help?" I asked.

Dad smiled like I'd offered him the key to the mint[36]. "I love you so much," he said. "You're ten thousand times better than I deserve, Ashes."

"Have a fry," I said, pushing my plate toward him. Dad took one. He seemed to have more of an appetite than I did.

"I had a thought," he said as he reached for my pickle. "Your mother keeps a couple hundred in cash at her place."

I didn't think either of us was supposed to know that.

[22] **to ponder sth.** = to think about sth. for a while
[23] **to do mental arithmetic** = to do calculations without writing them down
[24] **I'll be set for life** = I won't need to work again for the rest of my life
[25] **rice pudding** = a sweet food made from rice cooked with milk and sugar
[26] **booth** = table in a restaurant separated by two long seats with high backs
[27] **to take your pick** = to choose from alternatives
[28] **pickle** = (*US*) cucumber used in a hamburger
[29] **to pay off sth.** = pay for sth.
[30] **honey** = darling
[31] **I'm on my way to easy street** = (*infml*) I'm going to be rich
[32] **setback** = problem
[33] **to get itchy** = *here:* to get restless
[34] **give or take** = *here:* approximately
[35] **to twirl** = to make sth. move in circles
[36] **mint** = place where money is made (under government authority)

"In that pretty teapot her mother gave her," Dad said. "Unless she's changed her hiding place. I know she changed the locks when I moved out, so maybe she changed her hiding place as well."

Sometimes, when Mom wasn't home, I'd take the lid off the teapot and stare into it, imagining what I could do with two hundred dollars. I looked at Dad and realized he'd had those same fantasies. Well, why not. I was his daughter, after all.

"The money's still in the teapot," I said.

Dad grinned. "She's a wonderful woman," he said. "But she gets one idea and she never wants to change it."

"What do you want to do, Dad?" I asked. "Come into the apartment with me and take the money?"

"Oh no," he said, and he looked really shocked. "That would be robbery, Ashes. I would never steal from your mother. I've caused her pain enough."

I took a bite of burger. Dad ate some more fries.

"No, I just thought maybe you could borrow the money," he said. "Just for a day or two, until I straighten out[37] all my finances. Your mother would never know the difference. Unless there's an earthquake or the Martians[38] invade. I think we can gamble neither of those things will happen before Friday."

"You'll be able to pay her back by Friday?" I asked.

"You," Dad said. "I'd be borrowing the money from you. And I swear to you, Ashes, I'd have the money in your hands by Friday at the latest." He wiped his hand on his napkin and offered it to me as though to shake on the deal.

"Dad, I don't know," I said. "That's a lot of money. What if Mom finds out?"

"It's me she'd be angry at," Dad said. "Which is why she'll never find out. I wouldn't jeopardize[39] our time together, honey. You let me have the money tonight, I'll straighten out my little difficulty, and Thursday night, when your mom is out, I'll give you back what I owe you. No earthquakes, no Martians, no problem."

I looked at the clock on the wall behind Dad. "Mom'll be home soon," I said.

"You all through?[40]" he asked.

I nodded.

"Let's go, then," he said, the rice-pudding test long forgotten.

[…]

We drove back to Mom's in silence. Usually we talked.

Sometimes Dad sang one of his songs to me. For a moment, a cloud drifted past the moon and the sky turned greenish gray.

"Snow tomorrow," Dad said. "Maybe you'll get a snow day."

"Maybe," I said.

[…]

"You go up to the apartment," he said. "Take the money, and come right down. Then I'll drop you off in front of her place, like always, and she'll never know the difference."

[37] **to straighten sth. out** = to sort sth. out
[38] **Martians** = creatures from the planet Mars
[39] **to jeopardize** ['dʒepədaɪz] = to risk damaging sth. important
[40] **you all through?** = (*US*) Have you finished?

"What do I do if Mom's already there?" I asked.

"Just stay where you are," he said. "If you're not back here in ten minutes, I'll go home."

"All right," I said, and reached to unlock the door.

Dad touched me on my shoulder, gloved hand on winter coat.

"You're one in a million," he said to me. "The best daughter a man could dream of."

I got out of the car and ran over to the apartment. I took the elevator to the tenth floor and unlocked the door. The apartment was quiet. It always felt a little colder when Mom wasn't there. Even with the lights turned on, it seemed a little darker. I walked into the kitchen and turned on the light. The teapot was right where it belonged. I lifted its lid and stared at her emergency money. It was shaped like a little house, with a curtained window and a flowerpot on the windowsill. It was the sort of house I'd never lived in, probably never would with the amount of time it was taking Mom to finish her degree.

I stood over the teapot and stared at the money; Mom's emergency money. Her earthquake money. Her Martian money. Ten Andrew Jacksons[41] stared right back at me. They offered me no advice on what I should do.

I looked out the window and saw only ash gray sky. In the cold stillness of the night, I could hear my father's car keening[42] in the distance. "You're one in a million," it cried.

[41] **Andrew Jackson** = twenty dollar bill
[42] **to keen** = (*lit.*) to make a long high sound expressing pain or sadness

Analysis

C3 Compare the narrative perspective in "Ashes" to that in "Red". What differences do you notice? How might they affect the reader?

C4 Analyze how stylistic devices are used in lines 25–58. Illustrate the characters' feelings and relationships. Pay special attention to words relating to weather and nature and how the characters of mother and father are contrasted.

Skills
How to write a text analysis p. 83

Comment

C5 Ashes's father claims that "one good dream is worth a thousand flashlight batteries," in lines 57–58. Comment on this view.

Skills
How to write a comment p. 84–85

Checklist

- ✓ First explain how you understand the quotation.
- ✓ In your argumentation use your knowledge of Ashes's father to discuss what he might mean by it.
- ✓ Comment on it based on your own experience and convictions.
- ✓ Keep the tips from the checklist for "Red" in mind.

2 Childhood in retrospect

Getting started

A1 Look at the photos on pages 22 and 23. Write down one word for each photo that captures the atmosphere best.

1

2

3

A2 a) With a partner choose one of the seven photos. Imagine one of you is the child in the photo and the other is the parent who took the photo.
Write down what you feel and what goes through your mind. Consider the situation, the surroundings and the possible causes of your feelings.

b) Exchange your texts. Find out if child and parent interpret the situation in the same way. Give reasons for your view.

4

5

6

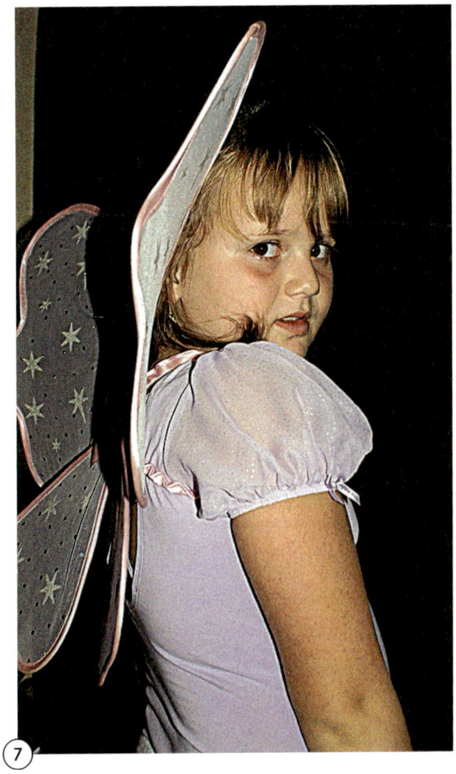

7

Practice section

Comprehension

> **Tip**
> *The "I" in a poem refers to an imagined unidentified speaker. This must not be confused with the poet. The speaker in a poem may also be referred to as the poetic persona.*

B1 Read the poem "We remember your childhood well" by Carol Anne Duffy.
State briefly what it is about. In order to do this task you need to

- look at the title of the poem. This may give you a clue about the theme.
- read the poem a few times to get an idea of the general situation.
- identify the speaker(s) and the addressee. The use of personal pronouns will help you find out who they might be.
- look at the lines highlighted in the poem. Find out what events they may refer to.

We Remember Your Childhood Well

Nobody hurt you. Nobody turned off the light and argued
with somebody else all night. The bad man on the moors
was only a movie you saw. Nobody locked the door.

Your questions were answered fully. No. That didn't occur.
You couldn't sing anyway, cared less. The moment's a blur, a Film Fun
laughing itself to death in the coal fire. Anyone's guess.

Nobody forced you. You wanted to go that day. Begged. You chose
the dress. Here are the pictures, look at you. Look at us all,
smiling and waving, younger. The whole thing is inside your head.

What you recall are impressions; we have the facts. We called the tune[1].
The secret police of your childhood were older and wiser than you, bigger
than you. Call back the sound of their voices. Boom. Boom. Boom.

Nobody sent you away. That was an extra holiday, with people
you seemed to like. They were firm, there was nothing to fear.
There was none but yourself to blame if it ended in tears.

What does it matter now? No, no, nobody left the skid marks[2] of sin
on your soul and laid you wide open for Hell. You were loved.
Always. We did what was best. We remember your childhood well.

[1] **to call the tune** = to be in a position of control or authority
[2] **skid marks** = black marks made by tyres when a car brakes suddenly

> **Language support**
> *might/may refer to sth.*
> *to suggest sth.*
> *to speculate on sth.*
> *to hint at sth.*
> *to imply sth.*
> *to allude to sth.*

> **Language support**
> *to disagree on sth./with so.*
> *to argue/quarrel about sth./with so.*
> *to contradict so./sth.*
> *to justify sth.*
> *to accuse so. of sth.*
> *to deny sth.*

B2 a) Look more closely at the content of the poem. Many events in the poem are deliberately left vague and open to interpretation and speculation.
Identify events the speaker and the addressee disagree on. Try to work out what might have happened.
Example: *"You couldn't sing anyway, cared less. The moment's a blur, a Film Fun laughing itself to death in the coal fire." (lines 5–6)*
These lines might refer to a time when the child was made fun of while singing. Possibly this was recorded on a home video.

b) Describe the attitudes the parents and the child assume towards each other in their memories of these events.

Analysis

B3 When you look at the **structure**, the **poetic devices** and the **tone** of a poem, you should consider the following aspects:

Info: Elements of poetry

element	definition	example
structure:		
stanza/verse	a section of a poem consisting of a group of lines	1st stanza of the poem on page 24: ll. 1–3; in this poem every other stanza begins with the same word.
enjambement	one line continuing to the next	"Nobody turned off ... all night." (ll. 1–2)
end-stopped line	the end of a line	
free verse	in a poem like this one without a fixed metre	"What you recall are impressions; we have the facts. We called the tune."
rhythm	the pace or "movement" of a poem. The rhythm is determined by the metre and by the length of sentences.	
metre	the pattern of stressed (/) and unstressed (˘) syllables. Free verse has no regular metre pattern.	free verse: no fixed metre "What you recall are impressions; we have the facts. We called the tune."
rhyme	the repetition of sounds usually at the end of two or more lines	"blur", "occur" (ll. 4–5)
rhyme scheme	the pattern created by the repetition of sounds at the end of lines	
tone:		
tone	the tone the author uses to convey his/her attitude towards the subject	ironic, serious, sentimental, humorous

element	definition and example	effect
poetic device:		
allusion	a reference to a familiar or famous historical or literary figure or event; e.g. "You wanted to go that day." (line 7)	These unexplained events create the feeling of secrecy.
anaphora	the repetition of identical words or phrases at the beginning of a sentence or a line; e.g. "Nobody hurt you. Nobody turned off the light ... Nobody locked the door." (ll. 1–3)	The repetition of "nobody" emphasizes the parents' denial of certain events.
antithesis	contrasting two opposites; e.g. "What you recall are impressions; we have the facts." (line 10)	The contrast of facts with impressions suggests that the parents are right.
ellipsis	leaving out words to avoid repetition; e.g. "Anyone's guess." (line 6)	This creates the impression that this poem is only one side of a conversation.
metaphor	a word or phrase used to describe so./sth. else which creates an image in the reader's mind and makes the description more powerful; e.g. "The secret police of your childhood" (line 11) – the parents	The image of the secret police creates a feeling of repression and fear.
onomatopoeia	words that sound like their meanings; e.g. "Boom. Boom. Boom." (line 12)	"Boom" suggests that the voices were loud and threatening.
parallelism	the repetition of sentence structure often used to contrast; e.g. "... look at you. Look at us ..." (line 8)	The difference between the parents and the child is underlined.
rhetorical question	a question which expects no answer; e.g. "What does it matter now?" (line 16)	The question suggests that the parents would prefer everything to be forgotten.

Skills
How to write a text analysis p. 83

Language support

The poem is made up of ...
Each stanza consists of ...
The poem is written in ...
There is no ...
The lines/rhythm of the poem ...

Language support

The line emphasizes ...
... tries to arouse the reader's interest
He/She criticizes/satirizes the situation by ...
The poet gives us a hint/clue/image of ...
The language used is ...

Language support

The persona's tone of voice implies ...
The feeling conveyed to the addressee ...
... wants to convince the addressee of ...

B4 a) Analyze the **structure** of the poem.

- Use the info-box on page 25 and describe the structure of "We remember your childhood well".
- Work with a partner. Talk about what effect the structure of the poem has on the reader. In order to do this read the poem out loud to each other.

b) Analyze the **poetic devices** used in the poem and explain how they underline the conflict between the parents and the child. In order to do this

- use the info-box for help and find examples in the poem.
- look at the choice of words. The poet uses a lot of "threatening" vocabulary like "hurt" (line 1) and "bad" (line 2). Find more examples in the poem. Explain the effect of the words on the reader.

c) Look at the poet's **tone**.

- Examine her judgement of the parents.
- State how she shows it.

Checklist

Structure:

✓ Stanzas: How many are there? Is there a regular pattern?
✓ Rhyme: Is there a rhyme scheme or is the poem written in free verse?
✓ Rhythm: Can you identify a particular pattern of stress or is the rhythm irregular? Do the lines stop at the end or are they run-on lines (enjambement)?

Language:

✓ Which poetic devices are used in the poem?
✓ What effect do they have on the reader?
✓ What effect is created by a particular choice of language?

Tone:

✓ What is the poetic persona's tone in the poem?
✓ What does it imply about his/her attitude towards the subject?

Comment/Creative writing

Skills
How to write a comment p. 84–85

Skills
How to write an informal letter p. 88

B5 Comment on the parents' assertion in the last line "We did what was best" taking into account whether this belief is typical of parents in general. Give examples and make sure you come to a conclusion.

B6 Choose a task:
Imagine you are the child from the poem on page 24, now grown-up. Write a letter to your parents.

- Express your own view of your childhood.
- Refer to at least one of the events mentioned in the poem.
- Mention your parents' behaviour.

Or:
As the child from the poem write a diary entry based on events mentioned in the poem.

Skills
How to write a diary entry p. 90

Getting to the point

Read both of the poems and choose one you would like to work on in more detail. Then do the tasks.

Comprehension

C1 In your own words briefly describe the speaker's childhood in the poem "My childhood" by jahanvi.

Analysis

C2 Analyze the structure and the language of the poem and explain how these two aspects underline its meaning.

Comment/Creative writing

C3 This poem depicts childhood in a different light from "We remember your childhood well". Say which of the two poems reflects your own childhood best. Give reasons for your choice.

C4 Write a poem about your own childhood using some of the rhetorical devices you have learnt about in this theme.

My Childhood

my childhood was the time when I was innocent
when the world seemed to be fair
when my universe was around my toys

my childhood was the time when I lived in dreams
when everyone was selfless
when everyone appeared to be a friend

my childhood was the time when my life was full of colours
when sorrows never knocked my door
when smile was gift presented to everyone

my childhood was the time when love was pure
when there were no obligations
when tenderness prevailed

my childhood was the time which is long gone
tears flow from my eyes when I go back in my childhood
my childhood will never come back but
the child in me will never go

Skills How to write a text analysis p. 83

Skills How to write a comment p. 84–85

Skills How to write creatively p. 86–87

Comprehension

C5 Describe the situation the speaker in this poem by Simon Armitage finds himself in.

Analysis

C6 Analyze the language of the poem and explain how it underlines the speaker's feelings towards his father.

Comment/Creative writing

C7 Comment on the last stanza of the poem. How far can the speaker be considered to accept defeat?

C8 Write a conversation between the speaker's father and mother after the former has discovered his son's earring.

My Father Thought It ...

My father thought it bloody queer[1],
the day I rolled[2] home with a ring of silver in my ear
half hidden by a mop of hair. "You've lost your head.
If that's how easily you're led
you should've had it through your nose instead."

And even then I hadn't had the nerve to numb
the lobe with ice, then drive a needle through the skin,
then wear a safety-pin. It took a jeweller's gun
to pierce the flesh, and then a friend
to thread the sleeper[3] in, and where it slept
the hole became a sore, became a wound, and wept[4].

At twenty-nine, it comes as no surprise to hear
my own voice breaking like a tear, released like water,
cried from way back in the spiral of the ear. If I were you,
I'd take it out and leave it out next year.

[1] **queer** = strange
[2] **to roll** = to walk with a swaying, unsteady motion
[3] **sleeper** = a small earring or stud worn to keep the hole of a pierced ear from closing
[4] **to weep** = to emit or run with drops of liquid

3

Life beyond school

Getting started

A1 a) Imagine you have just passed your final exams. Where do you go from here? Write down your plans for the immediate future.

b) Discuss your plans with a partner and talk about similarities and differences.

A2 A lot of young people choose to take a gap year after school. They spend some time travelling around the world, often to work or volunteer, but also to enjoy themselves. Here are three extracts from e-mail messages that gap year travellers (or "gappers") wrote home to their families.

a) Read the extracts. Summarize the gappers' different experiences.

b) Talk to a partner about how you would have felt and how well you would have coped in these situations.

c) Describe the image of "gap year" and "gappers" that is conveyed in the e-mails.

1.

This young student spent a year in northern Russia improving her language skills. The winter of 2005–6 was one of the coldest ever recorded there.

From: studentinrussia@gap.com Signature: None
To: parents@gap.com
Subject: cold winter

I know it is v dull to talk about the weather, but it is MINUS 30 degrees today, so I think I am allowed. All my shampoo on my shelf etc. freezes every night and children aren't allowed to go to school because they walk too slowly and tend to freeze to death before they get there. Nice. I am slightly worried as I walk at the speed of a lobotomized[1] snail, there is 5 inches of ice on the roads and my new boots have strayed far from their natural habitat[2] (the wilds of High St Ken.[3]). On the first day of unbelievable iciness I happily stepped outside and within minutes my mascara had frozen my eyelids closed and my nostrils had iced over, after another few minutes I lost all feeling in my extremities, so by the time I reached the Institute I couldn't see, smell or feel. I walk so slowly that I am often overtaken by octogenarian[4] babushkas[5] shuffling along in felt slippers[6] with massive sacks of turnips[7] on their backs. Every day Ludmilla smugly informs me that it is another 10 degrees colder than the day before and happily tells me how to notice the first stages of frostbite[8].

[1] **to lobotomize** = to remove a part of so.'s brain by a medical operation
[2] **habitat** = the area or environment in which so./sth. normally lives or grows
[3] **High St Ken.** = High Street Kensington in London
[4] **octogenarian** = a person between 80 and 90 years of age
[5] **babushka** = Russian: old woman, grandmother
[6] **felt slipper** = Filzpantoffel
[7] **turnip** = Rübe
[8] **frostbite** = a medical condition in which cold weather seriously damages your fingers, toes, ears or nose

2.

Politics rarely intrudes into the lives of our gappers, but when it does, it can be embarrassing. Imagine that your child was in Nepal and they reported back that everything was just fine – except that they had been seized by a group of revolutionary guerrillas.

From: gapperinnepal@gap.com Signature: None
To: parents@gap.com
Subject: what an experience

We first encountered the Maoists about a month into the placement. Somewhere along the line what actually happened got a bit distorted. To say we were held hostage[1] would be overshooting the mark[2], although technically it's true. We all went to get the 11 a.m. bus into Ghorabi, and as we approached the place where the bus sits and waits we were surrounded by six men, none older than us, brandishing[3] 1960's Kalashnikov rifles[4]. They told us to sit down (we did) and that we were not allowed to leave until the rally[5], which we had inadvertently stumbled upon, was finished.
It was scary, they were painfully young and they had guns which they chose to point at us. So for four hours we sat and listened and watched while these Maoists preached their message to the masses. After the initial fear wore off, it simply became a bit boring. We couldn't understand what was being said, and it lasted a long time. When it was finished we walked home, and that was that.

[1] **to be held hostage** = als Geisel gehalten werden
[2] **to overshoot the mark** = über das Ziel hinausschießen
[3] **to brandish** = to wave a weapon around in your hand
[4] **rifle** = a large gun
[5] **rally** = a gathering, a public meeting intended to inspire enthusiasm for a cause

3.

This young woman is a volunteer in Kenya and accompanies her pupils to an inter-school music competition:

From: volunteerinkenya@gap.com Signature: None
To: parents@gap.com
Subject: Kenyan kids

Next to the other school, our primary children look like a Kenyan version of the Bash Street Kids[1]. The neatness of the other competitors only made us more fiercely loyal to our little darlings, and the music teacher, Mr Wafula, said that we sounded like a hundred people cheering rather than three. I was also filled with maternal[2] pride when they came second, a feeling which surprised me as I spend most of my lessons confiscating ingenious catapults made from a hollow biro and an elastic band, unsticking small children from the wall in art lessons, or avoiding eagerly offered snotty hands.
They are also getting bolder and wander into the house without warning. This means it's not unusual to come out of the bedroom wearing nothing but a towel to find three small children in the kitchen trying to take apart the gas stove. I'm doing reading lessons to help a 4-year-old called Tracey, and it's going well. You may think that Tracey is an odd Kenyan name, but I teach Wayne, Brenda, Maureen, Kelvin, Brian and Eric. I'm also helping with a national art competition, although I had to explain to Mr Okingo that 'helping' was not the same as 'doing 20 entries myself and getting the children to write their names at the bottom', which is what he wanted me to do.

[1] **Bash Street Kids** = an ongoing comic strip in the British comic *The Beano*
[2] **maternal** = of a mother

A3 Together with a partner, act out a role play. One of you is the student who wants to go on a gap year, travelling to exotic countries, one of you is his or her mum/dad, who is rather worried about that idea.

Practice section

Pre-reading

B1 Read the heading of the article from *The Guardian* and speculate on what it is about.

Patrick Kingsley *The Guardian, 6 September, 2010*

Gap years: Wasted youth?

Ever wondered what students really get up to on their gap years? A report from the Full Moon Party in Thailand

Outside the Drop In bar on Kho Phangan, Thailand, 25 August 2010. Photograph for the Guardian by Sean Smith

Up and down the beach, young western men are unzipping their shorts and peeing into the Gulf of Thailand. Behind them, under the light of the full moon, thousands more shirtless, shoeless Europeans are massed outside 14 beachside bars, their knees bending awkwardly to a soundtrack of the Black Eyed Peas, Justin Bieber and generic drum'n'bass. And squeezed between the bars and the crowds are 35 wooden stalls, each selling plastic buckets filled with a litre's worth of vodka and Red Bull. The stalls are daubed with deeply dubious slogans, ranging from the lurid to the moronic. "No Bucket No Boom Boom", "Fuck My Buckets", "Everybody Fuck My Strong Buckets" – that kind of thing.

Welcome to the Full Moon Party, the largest beach rave in the world. Twenty-five years ago, this was a little-known hippy hang-out on the remote Thai island of Koh Phangan. Today, frequented every month by between 10,000 and 30,000 European youngsters, the all-night party is the ultimate destination on south-east Asia's "banana pancake" trail; a mecca for footloose gap-year tourists. This party scene, right here on this beach, is arguably the epitome[1], the pinnacle[2], of the modern gap-year experience. Three weeks ago, the chief executive[3] of the universities and colleges admissions service (UCAS)[4] declared to a Sunday newspaper that "the golden age of the gap year is over". Mary

[1] **epitome** = the best possible example of a particluar type of person or thing
[2] **pinnacle** = *here:* the most exciting part of so.'s life
[3] **chief executive** = the most senior manager in a company or organization
[4] **UCAS** = Universities and Colleges Admissions Service = an organization responsible for managing applications to almost all UK universities and colleges

Comprehension

B2 a) Read the article and check whether your speculations were right.

b) Describe the different experiences of the gap-year travellers in the article.

Skills
How to work with a dictionary
p. 101–102

Curnock Cook argued that while in the past "a gap year has been when young people take a nice break and go out and see the world", the period should now "be used in a focused way to support an application to the course or university you are targeting". In a year when the number of university applications – a record 660,000 – has dwarfed[5] the number of university places available – 450,000 – Curnock Cook may have a point.

But this is a point that has yet to trickle down, in practical terms, to the nation's school-leavers. In fact, the vast majority of gappers do not use their year-out in anything approaching a fashion that might – in the eyes of universities – be viewed as "constructive". Every year around 160,000 British school-leavers take a gap year before entering university. More than 80% of them, says Richard Oliver, chairman of trustees at Year Out, "just go off and travel independently without any real purpose. Sun, sand and sangria, as I call it." Indeed, the trend might even be away from the year of constructive good deeds that Curnock Cook might be thinking of – a trend towards increasingly mindless hedonism. [...]

Attempting to understand why they go, however, why this is the modern gap-year experience, is exactly what brings me to the Full Moon Party, surrounded by scores of topless teenagers urinating into the ocean to the words of the Black Eyed Peas' "I gotta feeling/That tonight's gonna be a good night/That tonight's gonna be a good, good night." What exactly is the lure of this beach to teenagers who are, after all, meant to be Britain's brightest? I'm here to find out. [...]

"You know what the worst thing about travelling is?" asks Londoner Jez, 19 years old, dressed in a vest, and approaching the end of his year out. He enlightens me: "TOURISTS." It's a slightly strange answer: we're sitting on the side of a dirt track near the centre of Had Rin, the main tourist town on Koh Phangan, and venue for tomorrow's Full Moon Party. Tourists are whizzing past every 30 seconds on mopeds belching out acrid fumes. [...] But Jez – a warm, welcoming guy – doesn't think of himself as a tourist: he's a backpacker. "Most of the people here are backpackers," he insists. "Backpackers are infinitely different to tourists. [...] All the people you've met while you're travelling will be here. It's just awesome."

[...] Hailey's gap-year experiences were slightly different to Jez's. She didn't go travelling at all, she says, but spent the entire period working in a hospital in order to enhance her application to medical school; a perfect exemplar of the kind of gap year favoured by Curnock Cook. In many ways, though, she wishes she'd chosen a more relaxed path. "I don't know if I should say this," she starts, pauses, then continues: "I was in a verbally abusive relationship for three years, which meant I had no self-confidence. And I turned into a bit of a slut on my gap year because I was really messed up in the head. And then I went to uni, and I thought, 'I don't want to be either of those people I've been, I want to be someone else.' So then I sort of[6] had three personalities. But coming out here on my own, having to go over and talk to people, having to be nice, not an asshole ... It's been great. It teaches you how to socialise properly. It makes you so much more confident. Coming out here, travelling on your own ..." She trails off, and then hurriedly starts again: "If I'd done the whole travelling on my own thing in my gap year, I would have been slightly less messed up[7] at uni." [...]

Up and down the beach, young western men are still unzipping their shorts and peeing into the Gulf of Thailand. Though I never took a gap year, never took the chance to either let my hair down like this, or do something more constructive, nothing that I've heard or seen here makes me want to join them.

[5] **to dwarf** = to make sth. seem small or unimportant
[6] **sort of** *(infml)* = somewhat, rather
[7] **messed up** *(infml)* = so. who is messed up has emotional or mental problems because unpleasant things have happened to them

Analysis

Identifying the type of newspaper article

B3 Identify what kind of newspaper article the text is. Use the definitions below.

Info: Types of articles
Articles can be distinguished by the way they are written and the purpose they serve.

1. Informative articles
Here the main focus is on providing factual information so that the article basically provides answers to *wh*-questions such as *who, what, where, when, why* and *how.*

2. Argumentative articles
In such articles the author clearly intends to influence the reader and his opinion by presenting arguments that are put forward to express a particular point of view.

3. Evaluative articles
In such articles the author provides a critical account of an event or a topic and tends to incorporate narrative and evaluative elements.

Note: Articles often have characteristics of more than one of the types described above.

Structure of a newspaper article

B4 Divide the article into units and identify the main function of each part.

Info: Structure of a newspaper article

1. Consider the **headline** and **sub-heading** as they clarify the topic and give you a clue as to whether the article is simply informative or includes the author's interpretation of events or a form of argumentation as well.
2. Look for an **introduction**, which may include the most important information (*who, what, where, when, why, how*) or consist of a paragraph that is meant to capture the reader's attention by providing an entertaining, emotive or critical lead into the text.
3. Read the **main part** of the text. Identify the main part's structure and the function of the individual paragraphs: is a paragraph more informative and fact-based or does it include the author's or someone else's opinion? Does the paragraph focus on facts (e.g. statistics, details of an event) or personal statements and examples?
4. Check whether there is a **concluding paragraph** that sums up the article's message or main points. Does it refer back to the beginning so that the article comes full circle?
5. Sometimes **photos, graphs** or **additional texts** may have been added to the article.

Distinguishing between fact and opinion

B5 a) Read the text again and identify passages that express facts and opinions. Write down examples with line numbers and explain why you consider them facts or opinions.

Info: Facts vs. opinions

1. An article usually contains a number of **facts**. A fact is something that is known to be true and can be proved to be so.
2. However, the author may also include his or her **opinion**, i.e. something that is a belief or judgement which others may or may not agree with according to their point of view.
3. If a text relies heavily on opinions, it is said to be **biased** and needs to be read critically.

b) Based on your findings in a), discuss whether the article is biased in the sense that the author's personal point of view is clearly stated. Describe the effect on the reader. The following questions may help you come to a conclusion:

Tip
For more information on bias look at page 43.

facts	opinions
• Do the facts represent just one point of view? • How are positive and negative facts balanced out? • To what extent do you feel that some facts have been omitted on purpose? If so, which ones might those be?	• Are some opinions presented as facts? • Has the author used opinions to persuade or influence the reader in a certain way? • Are facts and opinions linked so that they add up to an overall point of view of the text?

c) Reassess what kind of newspaper article this is. Use your findings from b) for support.

Language

B6 Analyze how the use of language expresses bias or neutrality on the author's part.

Skills
How to write a text analysis p. 83

Skills
How to improve your text p. 94–95

Info: Language

The reader's understanding of a topic can be influenced in many ways.

1. **Choice of words:**
   → use of comparatives and superlatives, e.g. "Britain's brightest (l. 65), "more constructive" (l. 113)
   → use of strong or emotive adjectives and verbs, e.g. "dwarfed" (l. 38), "mindless" (l. 55)
2. **Register:**
   → matter-of-fact and neutral language
   → formal and academic language
   → informal and colloquial language
3. **Stylistic devices:** e.g. repetition, enumeration, irony, exaggeration, metaphor
4. **Rhetorical strategies:**
   → to quote experts and authorities or to refer to research and statistics
   → to include personal statements of people affected by what is presented
   → to make claims (instead of arguments based on evidence, e.g. *No one can deny that …*)
   → to use humour, irony, ridicule

Comment

Skills
How to write a letter to the editor p. 89

Skills
How to improve your text p. 94–95

B7 Write a letter to the editor in which you comment on the way tourists and backpackers or "gappers" are presented in the article.

When writing a letter to the editor, you should follow the structure below.

• Don't use "Dear ...".	*Sir or Madam:*
• Start by naming the article you refer to and giving the reason for writing your letter. • State right away what you would like to praise/criticize about the article.	*Having read your 6 September article "...", I would like to/I feel the need to point out ...* *I am writing in response to your article "..." from ...* *As a firm believer in ... / As a supporter of ..., I totally agree / I see no reason why ...*
• Present your arguments in a structured form. • Refer to the original article, but do not quote. • Go beyond the article to explain why you share/oppose the author's point of view.	*It is beyond doubt that ...* *What you need to keep in mind is ...* *Your article raises the question whether ...* *The way I see it, ...* *Although I understand why ..., I cannot accept your overall conclusion that ...* *I think you are mistaken if you believe ...* *You overlook the fact that ...* *You are absolutely right when you say that ...*
• End your letter with a strong statement, e.g. a final appeal or a strong expression of your opinion.	*That is why I hope that you will keep drawing attention to ...* *Therefore, we should be careful ...* *Consequently, I strongly support your view ...*
• Close the letter by writing your name and place of residence.	*John Miller* *London, England*

Getting to the point

Pre-reading

C1 Study the picture, the caption and the advice box on the left. Explain what kind of article you expect from these first impressions.

Owen Henry, 19, of Waterford, Va., graduated from high school last year. Now he's working on the *Lady Maryland*, a tall ship, as a deckhand[1] during his gap year in Baltimore. He'll enroll this fall at Oberlin College.

By Mike Buscher for USA TODAY

[1] **deckhand** = so. who works on a ship doing jobs such as cleaning

"Gap year" before college gives grads valuable life experience

by G. Jeffrey MacDonald, Special for USA TODAY

How to be productive

For a productive year between high school and college:
– **Secure a place in college first.** Then defer enrollment for a year. This is less hectic than spending the gap year doing applications.
– **Have a plan.** Set goals and create structure to prevent depressing downtime at home.
– **Research programs.** If an organization can't recommend at least two alumni to discuss their experiences, don't sign up.
– **Respect your social needs.** The year represents a break with the crowd, so it's important to plan strategies for making new friends and staying in touch with old ones.
– **Plan ahead for health insurance.** Some policies won't cover adult-age dependents if they cease to be full-time students. Check your policy several months in advance, then explore temporary insurance if necessary.
Source: Center for Interim Programs, Princeton, N.J.

Worn-out high school seniors are getting fresh encouragement from a range of sources to take a break – a "gap year" – before plunging into college. But to be beneficial, it needs to involve more than rest and relaxation.

This spring, high schools in seven metropolitan areas hosted their first gap-year fairs to acquaint students with options for spending a year away from the academic treadmill. Earlier in the year, Princeton University announced plans to formalize a "bridge year" program for admitted students to do service work abroad before enrolling.

[...]

Though the concept may be new to many in the USA, it's an established tradition elsewhere. In the United Kingdom, for instance, about 11% of the 300,000 college-bound seniors take a gap year before enrolling. Australia puts up similar aggregate numbers in what's known Down Under as "going walkabout".

Reliable data for gap-year activity aren't available for the USA, but guidance counselors and college admissions officers say they're seeing a surge[2] of interest.

One contributing factor: The high-pressure senior year of high school increasingly leaves students drained and craving refreshment.

Also, counselors are coming to bless the gap-year option, and colleges increasingly are offering a deferred enrollment option as more and more "gappers" arrive on campus with enhanced focus, motivation and maturity — all of which bodes well[3] for their undergraduate years in college.

"Counselors are recognizing that there are many pathways to college," says David Hawkins, director of public policy and research at the National Association for College Admission Counseling. "They see that, if properly vetted, these opportunities could actually help students succeed in college."

[...]

Consultants agree gap years shouldn't be just "time off," and should instead be crafted with clear goals in mind.

But whether a gapper learns and grows more in a highly programmed environment than in one that's less predictable remains a topic open for discussion.

Some recommend adhering to a set of structured activities that minimize the likelihood of prolonged downtime at home or major pitfalls on the road.

"Most people need structure," says Holly Bull of the Center for Interim Programs. "Parents come to me halfway through a child's gap year and say, 'It's sort of falling apart here. We need more ideas or more structure.' So structure is important."

Others say that while the highly structured approach may be good for businesses that cater to gappers, too much "hand-holding" can hinder the maturation process that tends to happen in the absence of ample support systems.

"Unlike Europeans, (Americans') happiness to be handheld throughout the process creates demand for support services, orientation and premium products required to keep them safe and show them a good time," says Tom Griffiths, founder of gapyear.com. But "if you're not in a group, you get more out of it. It's just a fact that if you travel around the world on your own, you grow up."

Confidence from experience

U.S. gappers sing the praises of structured programs, but they also say they grew most when they had to live by their wits.

[...]

Owen Henry of Waterford, Va., opted in 2007 to take a gap year when he received a pile of college rejection letters. His goals for the year: to be challenged, gain work experience and clarify academic goals. He participated in a program for American gap-year students last fall at Oxford University, where he says he spent less than $10,000, and he decided on a career as an Arabic translator.

Since March, he has been handling two tons of sail as a deckhand on the Lady Maryland, a 104-foot-long tall ship and floating classroom in Baltimore. He gets room, board and $6.54 an hour. He has saved $1,600 of this for college, and he plans to enroll this fall at Oberlin College, to which he applied and was accepted during the gap year.

(Most experts recommend applying to colleges during senior year, getting accepted and then requesting a one-year deferral.)

"Feeling my hands cracking apart and being destroyed and slowly built up again with calluses[4]

[2] **surge** = a sudden increase in sth.
[3] **to bode well** = to be a sign that sth. good will happen
[4] **callus** = a hard thick area of skin caused by rubbing, especially on your hands and feet

was a slow and painful process," Henry says. But this was his first job, and he resolved, "I'm not quitting just because my hands are sore."

Learning from failure

[...]

Even mishaps can be a boon[5] by yielding[6] the very outcomes that a gap year is supposed to deliver.

Karl Haigler, author of The Gap Year Advantage: Helping Your Child Benefit From Time Off Before or During College, recalls a gapper who got malaria in Africa. "She had to cope, and she turned it into a positive. She said she learned to be an advocate because she had to advocate for herself to get health care."

Says Samer Hamadeh, co-founder of Vault.com, a career information company: "To be able to talk about a failure as an experience and how you learned from it — that's invaluable. So you can't go wrong. That's the bottom line. Just plan it, do it as a deferral (to college), have a goal and then go for it."

But figuring out how best to do a gap year is still a matter of balancing risks, potential benefits and personal interests.

In that mix, Bull says, students should do plenty of advance research and try to avoid potential nightmare situations, such as becoming ill without a solid support network in a developing country.

"You don't have to go through that as a parent or as a student," Bull says.

[5] **boon** = sth. useful that brings great benefits or makes your life easier
[6] **to yield** = to produce sth. useful

Comprehension

C2 Read the article published in 2008 and outline the reasons for the increase in the numbers of gappers and their experiences as described in the article.

Analysis

C3 Describe the author's attitude towards gap years and analyze the means he uses to support it.

Skills
How to write a text analysis p. 83

Comment

C4 Your gap year has been a negative experience for you.
Write a letter to the editor commenting on the views expressed in the article.

Skills
How to write a letter to the editor p. 89

4 The dangers of the Internet

Getting started

A1 a) Think about how much time you spend on the Internet and what you use it for. Note down your results.

b) Compare your notes in small groups.

Tip
It is usually the combination of visual elements and text in a cartoon that creates a humorous effect.

A2 Study the cartoon and say what makes it funny.

"I love our nights in together, just you, me, and our 756 friends."

A3 a) Write down reasons why people use chat rooms and why they are attracted to them. Consider possible problems and add them to your list.

b) Read the two extracts and look at the cartoon. Note down any additional aspects you can find. Then compare your results with a partner.

Extract 1 from "Amy" by Mary Hooper

[Amy (Buzybee) meets Zed in a chat room on the Internet.]

"It all started after I fell out with Louise and Bethany, really. It was falling out with them that made me find friends somewhere else, and the Internet seemed a good place to look.
I mean everyone wants friends, don't they?" [...]

[Soon they start chatting one to one outside the chat room and even exchange photographs.]

B: Love the photo. I've got it by my bed.
Z: Yours is GR8. You're a babe[1]!
B: Was yours taken in the office!
Z: Yeah. It was for the salesman of the week board. [...]

[1] **You're a babe** = you look fantastic

B: Have U ever been at the top?
Z: Loads of times. I'm brilliant at selling!
B: I'd be useless.
Z: Hey – U look GR8 in your photo, but it's only head shoulders. What about the rest of U!
B: What about it?
Z: Your figure?
B: I go in and out a bit!
Z: I need 2 know more than that if I'm going 2 get the full picture. I like 2 fantasise! So how about giving me your bust size?
B: 34.
Z: Cup size?
B: B.
Z: OK! Hang on a sec – I'm going to close my eyes and think about U. [...]
Z: How about us 2 getting together some time?
B: You mean meet up 4 real?
Z: Right. U could come down here 4 the day. Stay the night with me.

Extract 2 from "Fever of the Bone" by Val McDermid

[The police are investigating the murder of Jennifer Maidment.]

"According to Claire Darsie, her and Jennifer used Rigmarole[1] all the time. And Gary here's been able to pull up[2] a whole stack[3] of their chat room and IM[4] sessions."
"Anything useful?" [...]
"There's a lot of rubbish," Gary said. "The usual teenage chatter about X Factor and Big Brother. Pop stars and soap actors. Gossip[5] about their mates[6] from school. Mostly they're talking to other kids in their class, but there are some outsiders from other areas of Rigmarole." [...]
"And then it gets really interesting," Gary said [...].
"This was five days ago."

Jeni: Wot do u mean, zz?
ZZ: Evry1 has secrets, things theyr ashamed of. Things u'd die if ur crew new about.
Jeni: I don't. My best friend nos everything about me.
ZZ: That's wot we all say and we all lying.

[...] "... then ZZ pulls Jennifer into a private IM session. Here we go[7]."

ZZ: I wanted 2 talk 2 u in priv8.
Jeni: Y?
ZZ: cuz I no u hav a BIG secret.
Jeni: U no more than me then.
ZZ: sumtimes we don't know wot our own secrets r. Bt I no a secret tt u wd not want anybody else to no.
Jeni: I don't know wot u r on about[8].
ZZ: b online 2moro same time & we'll talk abt it sum more.

1 **Rigmarole** = fictional chat room/ social network
2 **to pull up sth.** = *here:* to find sth.
3 **a stack of** = a lot of
4 **IM session** = instant messaging
5 **gossip** = conversation about unimportant subjects
6 **mate** *(infml)* = friend
7 **here we go** = here it is
8 **wot u r on about** = what you are talking about

Practice section

Comprehension: cartoons

B1 Look at the cartoon "The Dangers of the Internet" below. Write down in one sentence why Colin uses the Internet and what the consequences are.

Analysis: cartoons

Skills
How to work with cartoons p. 92

B2 When analyzing a cartoon, you have to follow these steps:
- Identify the main visual and textual elements: caricature, caption, focal point, etc.
- Explain the effect these elements create.
- State the cartoonist's message and say what makes the cartoon funny.

a) Analyze the cartoon. The first sentence of your analysis should sum up the main idea of the cartoon. You can use your sentence from B1.

b) Copy the grid below. Match the visual and textual elements in the grid with their descriptions in the green and effects in the blue boxes.

text element: headline

text element: caption

explains what happened to the character while he was checking his e-mails

the title of the cartoon

childish clumsy writing

red

a character of unspecific age with thick glasses, an unathletic figure and old-fashioned clothes sitting at his computer; facial expression is difficult to describe as one cannot see his eyes

visual element: caricature: focal point in this cartoon

visual element: dominant colours

visual element: text font

illustrates the pitfalls of indiscriminate Internet use

suggests that he is a nerd, i.e. a boring person who is socially isolated; his goggle-type glasses and his hanging cheeks imply frustration and ignorance

specifies the message of the cartoon

indicates lack of maturity or intelligence

symbolizes danger

terms: visual elements	description	effect
dominant colours	red	symbolizes danger
…		
terms: text elements		
…		

[1] C-reg Vauxhall /ˌsiːredʒˈ vɒksɔːl/ = ein Opel Baujahr 08/1985 bis 07/1986

B3 a) Have a look at the cartoons below and write down in one sentence what each one is about (introductory sentence).

b) Choose one of the cartoons and find two or three other students who picked the same one. Follow the steps in the checklist to prepare your analysis.

c) Use the information you collected in your group to write a complete analysis on your own.

Language support
to suggest
to indicate
to depict
to imply
to show
to point towards
to visualize
to represent
to illustrate
to underline
to specify
to symbolize

Checklist
- ✓ State the topic dealt with in the cartoon in one sentence (introduction).
- ✓ Identify the most important visual and textual elements and describe them.
- ✓ Explain their effects.
- ✓ Consider what makes the cartoon humorous.
- ✓ State the cartoonist's message.
- ✓ Use appropriate vocabulary. Look at the language support box.

Skills
How to write a text analysis p. 83

"But... your Facebook profile says you're a vegetarian!"

1

2

"But, sweety, why don't you just read my blog, like everyone else?"

3

IT WAS AN AWKWARD MOMENT AS MAGGIE WALKED IN AND DISCOVERED BOOMER'S SECRET ONLINE IDENTITY

4

Comprehension: non-fictional texts

B4 Read the article "NJ student's suicide illustrates Internet dangers" by Geoff Mulvihill and Samantha Henry and state the authors' attitude towards the Internet in one or two sentences.
In order to do this follow these steps:
- Look at the headline and say what it suggests about the theme of the article.
- Find and note down any parts of the text in which the authors state their attitude or reveal their stance.

The Washington Post

NJ student's suicide illustrates Internet dangers

By GEOFF MULVIHILL and SAMANTHA HENRY

PISCATAWAY, N.J. (AP) – The shocking suicide of a college student whose sex life was broadcast over the Web illustrates yet again the Internet's alarming potential as a means of tormenting others and raises questions whether young people in the age of Twitter and Facebook can even distinguish public from private. Cruel gossip and vengeful acts once confined to the schoolyard or the dorm can now make their way around the world instantly via the Internet, along with photos and live video.

"It's just a matter of when the next suicide's going to hit, when the next attack's going to hit," said Parry Aftab, a New Jersey lawyer who runs the website WiredSafety.

Last week, Rutgers University freshman Tyler Clementi jumped to his death from the George Washington Bridge after his roommate and another classmate allegedly used a webcam to secretly broadcast his dorm room sexual encounters with another man. The two classmates have been charged[1] with invasion of privacy, with the most serious charges carrying[2] up to five years in prison.

The suicide of Clementi, a shy, gifted 18-year-old violinist, shocked and disturbed gay rights activists and others on campus. "Had he been in bed with a woman, this would not have happened," said Rutgers student Lauren Felton, 21, of Warren, N. J. "He wouldn't have been outed via an online broadcast, and his privacy would have been respected and he might still have his life."

The Associated Press found at least 12 cases in the U.S. since 2003 in which children and young adults between 11 and 18 killed themselves after falling victim to some form of "cyber-bullying" – teasing, harassing or intimidating with pictures or words distributed online or via text message.

In probably the best-known case, 13-year-old Megan Meier of Daddenne Prairie, Mo., hanged herself in 2006 after she received messages on MySpace – supposedly from a teenage boy – cruelly dumping[3] her. An adult neighbor was later found guilty of taking part in the hoax[4], but the conviction was overturned[5].

Earlier this year, 17-year-old Alexis Pilkington of West Islip, N.Y., who had landed[6] a college soccer scholarship, killed herself after receiving a stream of nasty messages.

Gregory Jantz, founder of A Place of Hope, a Seattle mental health care center, said young people who use the Internet to spread something damaging about others often don't realize how hurtful it can be because many of them have grown up in a world[7] that has blurred the line between public and private.

"Our kids are in a different zone now," Jantz said. Aftab said young people who would never bully someone face to face do it online in part because of the often-false sense of anonymity that the Internet provides[8]. "They'll also jump on because they don't want to be the next target," Aftab said.

In Clementi's case, prosecutors said that his roommate, Dharun Ravi of Plainsboro, N.J., and Molly Wei of Princeton, N.J., both 18-year-old freshmen, transmitted a live image of Clementi having sex on Sept. 19 and that Ravi tried to

[1] **to charge so. with sth.** = *here*: jdn. wegen einer Sache anklagen
[2] **to carry** = *here*: nach sich ziehen
[3] **to dump so.** = to end a romantic/sexual relationship with so.
[4] **hoax** = Täuschung
[5] **to overturn** = *here*: to say officially that sth. is wrong and change it
[6] **to land sth.** = *here*: to gain sth.
[7] **a world that has blurred the line between public and private** = a world where you can no longer tell the difference between public and private
[8] **to provide sth.** = to make sth. available

webcast a second encounter on Sept. 21, the day before Clementi's suicide. Ravi's lawyer and a lawyer believed to be representing Wei did not return calls.

The mourning[9] continued at Rutgers; in Ridgewood, the suburban New Jersey town where Clementi grew up and attended high school; [...] Childhood friend Mary Alcaro, who played in a summer music academy with him, said Clementi had been destined[10] for greatness. "I've never heard anyone make a violin sing the way he did," she said in an e-mail. [...]

Students at West Windsor-Plainsboro Regional High School, from which Ravi and Wei graduated[11], remembered them as nice people who were not in any way homophobic. Ravi had gay friends, said Derek Yan, 16, a junior. Yan said he chatted online with Ravi about what college life was like, and Ravi "said he was lucky to have a good roommate. He said his roommate was cool."

[9] **mourning** = process of showing great sadness after so.'s death
[10] **destined for sth.** = certain to do sth.
[11] **to graduate** = to finish your studies at a high school

Analysis: non-fictional texts

B5 Read the article again. Identify and explain the means the authors use to convey their attitude. When analyzing the authors' intention/point of view, you have to take these aspects into consideration:

- choice of language/words that trigger(s) associations; e.g. the words "shocking", "alarming", "tormenting", "vengeful", "cruel" imply danger;
- quotations to give weight to the arguments, i.e. citing expert opinions or eyewitnesses; e.g. *"The statement of a New Jersey lawyer lends authenticity to the authors' message."*
- facts and figures to back up the arguments by giving evidence;
- appealing to emotions and awakening human interest; e.g. the terrible loss caused by cyber-bullying and the resulting suicide.

a) Find more examples of these aspects in the text.

b) Assess how far the author's point of view is biased.

Skills
How to write a text analysis p. 83

Language support
one-sided, neutral, objective, subjective, (un)prejudiced, (im)partial, predisposed, biased, unbiased

Language support
The author expresses in a ... way
He/She makes a case for/against ...
He/She favours ...
He/She is in favour of ...
He/She is prejudiced against/towards/ argues for/against ...
He/She discriminates ...
He/She indirectly attacks ...
The underlying attitude is ...

Info: Bias

Definition of bias

Bias is a prejudice in favour of or against one thing, person, or group. It is a tendency to hold a certain point of view at the expense of other alternatives.

If an article is biased, it means that information is presented in a one-sided way based on a personal opinion rather than facts.

Detecting bias

- in the headline of an article;
- in the choice of information for an article: what facts/statistics are mentioned/not mentioned, numbers and statistics can be exaggerated or played down in order to influence the reader;
- in the choice of photos and their captions, e.g. photos can flatter a person or ridicule them;
- in the names and descriptions of people indicating bias, e.g. terrorist, ex-convict, call girl;
- in the choice of words. This can be a source of bias. For example, many negative expressions will influence the reader in a particular way.

Comment

B6 Discuss which of the cartoons in B3 on page 41 best illustrates the message of the article. Give reasons.

Skills
How to write a comment p. 84–85

Getting to the point

Comprehension

Skills
How to write a summary p. 82

C1 Read the article "How dangerous is the Internet for children?" by David Pogue and summarize the main points.

Analysis

Skills
How to write a text analysis p. 83

C2 Analyze the cartoon on page 45 and explain how its message is conveyed.

C3 Analyze the author's point of view in the article and explain the means used to underline it.

Comment

Skills
How to write a comment p. 84–85

C4 Assess to what extent both the cartoon and the article represent a biased approach towards the Internet.

How dangerous is the Internet for children?

A few years ago, a parenting magazine asked me to write an article about the dangers that children face when they go online. As it turns out[1], I was the wrong author for the article they had in mind[2].

The editor was deeply disappointed by my initial draft. Its chief message was this: "Sure, there are dangers. But they're hugely overhyped by the media. The tales of pedophiles luring children out of their homes are like plane crashes: they happen extremely rarely, but when they do, they make headlines everywhere. […]"

My editor, however, was looking for something more sensational. […] So the editor sent me the contact information for several parents of young children with Internet horror stories, and suggested that I interview them. One woman, for example, told me that she became hysterical when her eight-year-old stumbled[3] onto a pornographic photo. She told me that she literally dove[4] for the computer, crashing over a chair, yanking[5] out the power cord and then rushing her daughter outside.

You know what? I think that far more damage was done to that child by her mother's reaction than by the dirty picture.

Now, I realize that not everybody shares my nonchalance[6]. And again, it's not hard to find scattered anecdotes about terrible things that happen online.

But if you live in terror of what the Internet will do to your children, I encourage you to watch this excellent hour long PBS "Frontline" documentary. It's free, and it's online in its entirety. The show surveys the current kids-online situation – thoroughly, open-mindedly and frankly.

Turns out I had it relatively easy writing about the dangers to children under age 12; this documentary focuses on teenagers, 90 percent of whom are online every single day. They are absolutely immersed in chat, Facebook, MySpace and the rest of the Web; it's part of their ordinary social fabric to an extent that previous generations can't even imagine.

The show carefully examines each danger of the Net. And as presented by the show, the sexual-predator thing is way, way[7] overblown[8],

[1] **as it turns out** = wie es sich herausstellt
[2] **to have sth. in mind** = an etwas denken
[3] **to stumble onto sth.** = to find sth. by accident
[4] **dove** = *(US)* simple past form of dive
[5] **to yank** = to pull sth. with a lot of force
[6] **nonchalance** = feeling relaxed and not worried
[7] **way, way** = *(infml)* by a very large amount
[8] **overblown** = made to seem more important than it really is

just as I had suspected. Several interesting interview transcripts accompany the show online; the one with producer Rachel Dretzin goes like this:

"One of the biggest surprises in making this film was the discovery that the threat of online predators is misunderstood and overblown. The data shows that giving out personal information over the Internet makes absolutely no difference when it comes to a child's vulnerability to predation." (That one blew my mind[9], because every single Internet-safety website and pamphlet hammers repeatedly on this point: never, ever give out your personal information online.)

"Also, the vast majority of kids who do end up having contact with a stranger they meet over the Internet are seeking out that contact," Ms. Dretzin goes on. "Most importantly, all the kids we met, without exception, told us the same thing: They would never dream of meeting someone in person they'd met online."

Several teenagers interviewed in the story make it clear that only an idiot would be lured unwittingly into a relationship with an online sicko[10]: "If someone asks me where I live, I'll delete the 'friend'. I mean, why do you want to know where I live at?" says one girl.

Fearmongers[11] often cite the statistic, from a 2005 study by the Crimes Against Children Research Center, that 1 in 7 children have received sexual propositions while online. But David Finkelhor, author of that report, notes that many of these propositions don't come from Internet predators at all. "Considerable numbers of them are undoubtedly coming from other kids, or just people who are acting weird online," he says.

As my own children approach middle school, my own fears align[12] with the documentary's findings in another way: that cyber-bullying is a far more realistic threat. Kids online experiment with different personas, and can be a lot nastier in the anonymous atmosphere of the Internet than they would ever be in person (just like grown-ups). And their mockery[13] can be far more painful when it's public, permanent and written than if they were just muttered in passing in the hallway.

In any case, watch the show. You'll learn that some fears are overplayed, others are underplayed, and above all, that the Internet plays a huge part in adolescence now. Pining[14] for simpler times is a waste of time; like it or not, this particular genie is out of the bottle[15].

[9] **it blew my mind** = it impressed me very much
[10] **sicko** = so. who likes things that most other people find shocking
[11] **fearmonger** = so. who creates fear
[12] **to align with sth.** = to match or fit with sth.
[13] **mockery** = Spott
[14] **to pine for sth.** = to be sad because you want sth. you can't have
[15] **this genie is out of the bottle** = it's no longer possible to go back to the old state of affairs on this matter

5 Media and friendship

Getting started

A1 a) Collect ways of communicating with your friends. List the uses teens have for electronic media.

b) Compare your findings in class and use them to develop a questionnaire about how you communicate with your friends.

I am ( ) a boy. ( ) a girl.

		yes	*no*
1	*I regularly meet my friends in the afternoon/evening and at the weekend.*		
	…		

I am ( ) a boy. ( ) a girl.

		often	*sometimes*	*never*
1	*I chat with my friends on Facebook.*			
	…			

c) Conduct a class survey.

d) Point out significant results of the survey and explain them.

Skills
How to analyze statistics
p. 96–97

Language support
The horizontal/vertical axis shows …
There is a sharp/rapid/slow/… increase/decline in the number of …
… is distributed evenly/unevenly among …
The number of … reaches a peak/remains constant/…
Nearly … % of …
About a third/quarter of …
The majority / minority of …

A2 a) Look at the statistics on Facebook below and describe them.

b) Explain what they tell you about the development and relevance of Facebook worldwide.

c) Choose one of these Internet research tasks:
1. Find out what the figures for Facebook and other social networking sites are today. Point out how the use of social networking sites has developed in recent years.
Or:
2. Find out about Mark Zuckerberg, how he started Facebook and how his career has developed.

d) Present your results to the class. Discuss whether Zuckerberg deserves the title "Person of the Year" which he was awarded by TIME magazine in 2010.

The March to a Billion

As Facebook has opened its doors to more users, its membership has soared

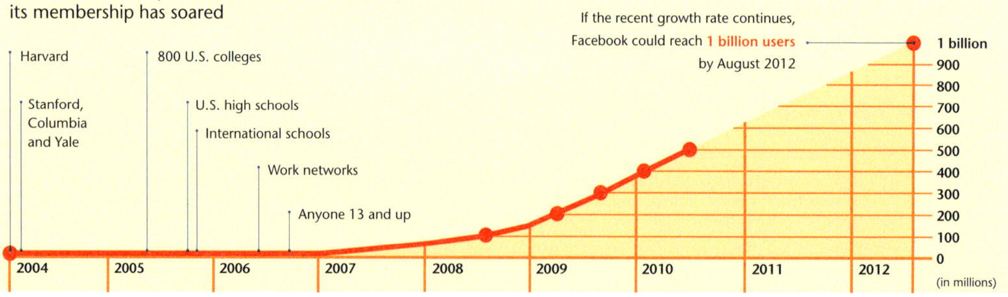

Friends of All Ages

The site now attracts sizable chunks of both young and middle-aged users

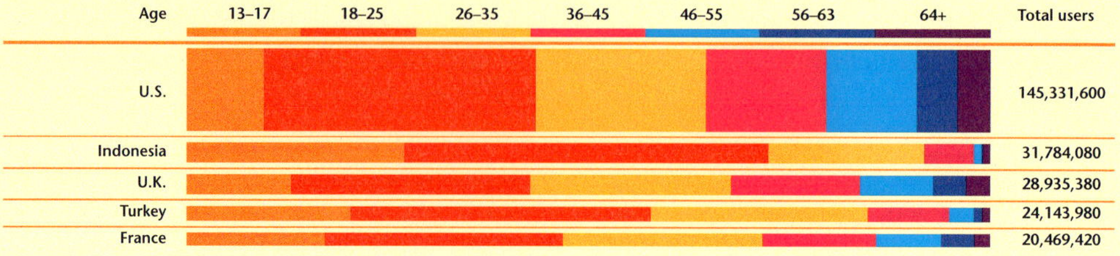

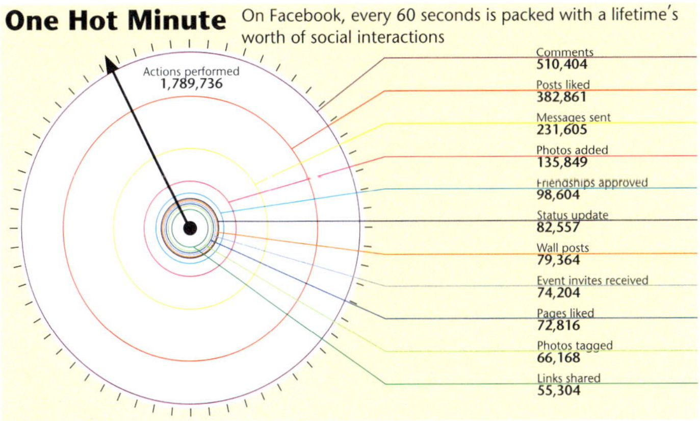

A3 a) Divide the class into two groups. Read the two texts on the question "Will Facebook conquer the world?" Each group concentrates on one text, either A or B. Make notes on the arguments put forward in favour of/against the extensive use of Facebook.

b) Add more arguments of your own.

c) In class, debate the statement "Making and keeping friends is impossible without Facebook." Note: You shouldn't present your own opinion but stick to the position of your article. Take a vote before the debate on how you see the issue.

d) After the debate, take another vote on the statement in class and discuss whether the debate has changed your view.

(A) *Daily Telegraph, Shane Richmond, 04 Jan. 2011*

[...] Facebook is still growing – at the rate of 700,000 people a day. It's closing in[1] on 600 million users, and as more join, the network becomes more powerful. Its members aren't just chatting and sharing photos, they are also playing games, reading the news and keeping up with famous people. Facebook Places lets them share their location with friends; Facebook Messages aims to replace our email accounts; and the Facebook experience is now available on more than two million websites. [...]

Facebook is more than just a website; it's a mini version of the web. Just as Google dominated the past decade, so Facebook could dominate the coming one. The difference between Facebook and Google is that the latter was only ever a starting point. Facebook is, for many users, the starting point and the destination.

Facebook hasn't just conquered the web, it's becoming a web of its own. [...]

(B) *Daily Telegraph, Will Heaven, 04 Jan. 2011*

[...] At the New Year's Eve house party I went to, the response to camera flashes could be heard over the din. "Can we all agree," one girl yelled, "that no one puts these photos on Facebook?" By midnight, the request made perfect sense. Who would want to risk sharing the evening – such as it was – with the entire online world?

For young Facebook users, that is the greatest concern: lack of privacy. The social networking website's Terms of Service are opaque[2]. And even if you manage to understand them, the "privacy" is often an illusion.

While developers quietly delve into your likes and dislikes, all you need to do is post a goofy picture online and before long your trendiest aunt (it was too rude not to accept her "friend request") has emailed it to your parents. Worse still, a friend from work could spot it – and suddenly, seen out of context by other colleagues, a photo lands you in serious trouble. [...]

[1] **to close in on so./sth.** = to move nearer to so./sth.
[2] **opaque** = *here:* difficult to understand

Practice section

Pre-viewing

B1 "The social network" is a film about Mark Zuckerberg and the development of Facebook. Imagine you are a team of film directors. In groups use the information you have compiled in A2 to plan the opening scene. Outline the scene and present your ideas to the class or to another group.

Comprehension

DVD

B2 The film "The social network" starts in a Harvard bar with a conversation between Mark and his girlfriend Erica, in which Mark's ambition to make it into the exclusive circles of Harvard becomes obvious; Mark is ditched by his girlfriend who claims that his problem is "not being a nerd but an asshole".

a) Watch extract 1 (5.14 min–8.30 min) which is part of the opening scene of the film, the exposition. Describe how this scene is used to introduce the topic, the setting and the main characters. Pay attention to what expectations are raised.

b) Compare the beginning of the film to your own ideas in B1. Point out the differences and explain what the directors of "The social network" might want to communicate by their particular opening.

B3 Watch the sequence again and describe the music that accompanies it. Consider how the combination of music and lighting is employed to create a special atmosphere. With a partner discuss what feelings this evokes in you.

Language support: film	
acoustic effects/music	**visual effects/lighting**
Rhythm and pace: • slow, fast • frantic • repetitive, monotonous *Mood:* • cheerful, playful • melancholic, sad, hesitant • sentimental, yearning • soothing, comforting • hopeful, promising • aggressive, threatening, scary, eerie • romantic, dramatic	• dark, gloomy • brilliant, blinding, bright • hazy, soft, shady

Analysis

Filmic devices

B4 Making a film also means using special filmic devices that carry meaning. This "film language" is created by the use of camera position or movement and by editing.

a) Read the definitions of different filmic devices and match them with the film stills on page 50. Be careful: not all definitions have a photo that goes with them. At the same time some stills may be labelled with two expressions.

b) Explain what the stills reveal about the relationships of the people presented. Consider how relationships or lack of relationships (distance, closeness, loneliness, isolation, superiority) are presented.

Info: Filmic devices and definitions

filmic device	definition
camera range / shot size	the distance between the camera and the object filmed
long shot	provides a view of the situation or setting from a distance
medium long shot	shows a person or people in interaction with their surroundings
full shot	gives a view of the entire figure of a person to show action or to give an impression of a constellation of characters
medium shot	shows a person down to the waist, often used to present two people in conversation
close-up	a full-screen shot of a person's face to show emotions revealed by their facial expression; it can also be used to draw attention to an object that is of particular interest to the plot or has a symbolic function
establishing shot	gives an overall impression of the location at the beginning of a scene
camera angle	the point of view of a camera
high angle shot	the camera looks down on the object so that it seems smaller, less important or inferior
low angle shot	the camera looks up at a person so that people seem more important, powerful or even intimidating as it shows them in a superior position
eye-level shot / straight-on angle	the camera looks straight at the person: this may suggest a neutral view, however, it can also mean that two people who are not on the same level for some reason (e.g. wealth, age, academic standing, social class) are presented as equal to each other
point-of-view	
point-of-view shot	assumes the perspective of one of the characters so that we seem to look through his/her eyes
over-the-shoulder shot	often used to present two people in conversation: you are looking straight at one person from behind the second person when it is important to reveal the reaction to what is being said
reverse angle shot	a sequence of point-of-view shots in which the perspective changes from one speaker to the other

filmic device	definition
camera movement	
panning shot	the camera moves horizontally, i.e. to the left or to the right
tilting shot	the camera moves vertically, i.e. upwards or downwards
tracking shot	the camera follows a person or an object
zooming in / zooming out	a stationary camera seems to move closer to or further away from the object, thereby focussing on it or showing it in its surroundings

1

2

3

4

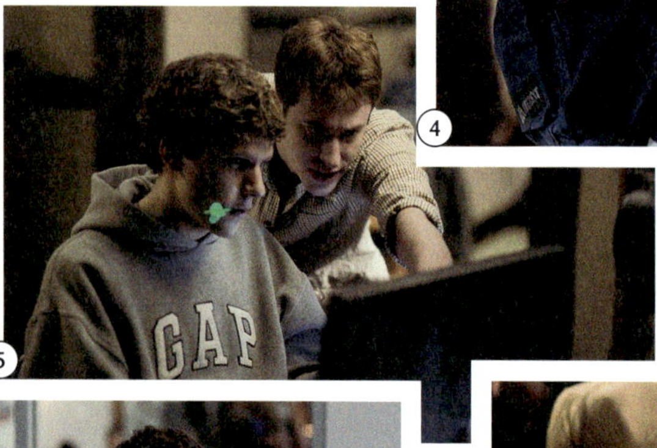

5

6

7

8

DVD

B5 a) Watch extract 1 from B2 again and identify the filmic devices.

b) Consider the filmic devices and explain their respective function within the framework of the film. What do they tell you about the setting, what about the character and his feelings?

c) It may help you to work with a viewing grid:

- Divide the sequence into different parts and label them.
- Note down specific filmic devices for each part. You can't note down every single change in camera position or camera angle, but some devices stand out and have an obvious function.

Viewing grid

scene	*action/picture content*	*filmic devices*	*function/effect/meaning*
1 The thirsty student			
2 Out on the street			
3 On the campus			
4 Kirkland House	*Mark running up stairs to door of "his" house/dorm*	*tilting up to name*	*high expectations, haven*
5 "Home"		*close-up/point-of-view shot of open fridge and beer*	*Mark needs some intoxication to get over his hurt feelings*

B6 Use your notes to outline how the director uses filmic devices to create an atmosphere of anticipation and to set the stage for the development of the plot, i.e. the creation of Facebook. This checklist will help you.

Checklist

Analyzing a film scene

✓ Remember to write a meaningful introduction to your analysis. Refer to the question.

✓ Don't present your findings in chronological order. Try to find groups of devices and explain them in context.

✓ Always identify a filmic device with reference to the picture content and explain why it is used; e.g. "The director uses a close-up of Mark to show the character's feelings of frustration and pent-up humiliation."; "Point-of-view shots of the beer in the fridge and of the computer are used to reveal Mark's focus – these are the two things that will keep him company and help him get over his disappointment."

✓ Always provide an interpretation of the filmic device you have spotted.

✓ Come to a meaningful conclusion that sums up your findings.

Language support: film

The director ...	makes frequent / occasional use of device x.	
The character(s) ... Their relationship ...	is / are shown / presented / ...	in a x shot by a panning / tilting camera.
Device x ...	is used ... is employed ...	to reveal ... / to expose ... to make clear ... / to highlight ... to emphasize ... / to underline ... to suggest ... / to criticize ... to ridicule ... / ...

Comprehension

DVD

B7 Before starting work on Facebook, Mark Zuckerberg created a programme called Facemash while studying at Harvard. Hacking into the university's databases, he retrieved the female students' photos and programmed Facemash in such a way that two random girls' photos were put side by side, asking the users to click on the girl who they thought looked better.

Watch extract 2 from "The social network" (8.34 min–13.52 min) and describe how Mark and his friends spend the evening compared to the students at the Phoenix club house.

Analysis

Editing

B8 Read the info-box below and match the functions (1–4) with the types of editing (A–D):

1. e.g. to present two sides of the same plot development, to speed up the action, to give the viewer additional information
2. to explain why a character is in a particular situation or how a problem came about
3. to hint at what the characters may be about to experience and show the effects their present actions can have
4. to link two subsequent scenes more closely in a way that supports the plot-based connection

Info: Editing

Every film is composed of **shots**. The beginning and end of a shot are marked by **cuts**, i.e. the change from one image to another one. Shots can be very short or – if the camera films without any interruption – long. In modern films, there are often a lot of cuts so that shots that deal with the same part of the plot form a **sequence**.
The way shots are linked is referred to as **editing** or **montage**, which is usually done in a specific way to establish a meaningful relationship between the individual shots.
Typical examples of shots are:

types of editing	definition	function
A flashforward	a scene that shows what may happen in the future and thus interrupts the chronological order of the plot	
B flashback	a scene that shows what happened in the past and thus interrupts the chronological order of the plot	
C cross-cutting / parallel action	combining shots of two or more scenes which are usually taking place at the same time	
D match cut	two scenes that are connected by visual or acoustic means, e.g. a door is closed in one scene and opened in the following scene in a different context, someone is crying at the end of the first and the beginning of the second scene	

DVD

Language support:

The sequence includes a ... to show ...
The scene is followed by a ... in which ...
In order to link ... a ... is used in the form of ...
The director uses ... to show ... while ...
In this sequence, ... is used to emphasize/contrast/... that ...

B9 a) Identify the kind of editing that is used in extract 2 from the film (8.34 min–13.52 min).

b) Explain its effect on the viewer.

B10 a) Divide the class into two groups. One half of the class concentrates on what is going on in Mark's dorm, the other one on what is happening at the party at the Phoenix club. Concentrate on the editing and the points below (see info-box) and make notes in a grid:

aspect	*function/effect*
characters and character constellation: *– ...* *– ...*	

Info: Other relevant aspects when comparing scenes

When looking at the editing or when comparing two scenes, one should pay special attention to further differences or similarities between the scenes which may help to link or to contrast the scenes, such as:

- characters and character constellation
- actions
- objects (often with symbolic meaning)
- visual effects (e.g. lighting, use of particular colours) and acoustic effects

b) Compare your notes within your group and add what you have missed.

c) Form mixed groups with two experts from each side and present your findings to each other. Write down the key points of the other group.

d) Use your notes to analyze how filmic devices and other techniques are used to combine and contrast what is going on in Mark's dorm and at the party.

Comment/Creative writing

Skills
How to write a letter to the editor p. 89

B11 Read the article from *The Harvard Crimson*, the Harvard University's newspaper that reports on Facemash and the reactions to it. Write a letter to the editor in which you give your opinion on Facemash and the reactions to it.

Hot or Not? Website Briefly Judges Looks

By **Bari M. Schwartz**, *CONTRIBUTING WRITER* *Published:* Tuesday, November 04, 2003

Harvard students often compete in the classroom, but for at least a few hours this weekend, only one thing helped them make the grade—their looks.

[...] a website created by Mark E. Zuckerberg [...] gave students a chance to rate their peers using ID photos taken from online House facebooks[1].

"Were we let in for our looks? No. Will we be judged on them? Yes," proclaimed the site, which Zuckerberg has now taken offline.

Zuckerberg, a computer science concentrator[2], said he created the site – www.facemash.com – by hacking into House online facebooks and compiling ID photos onto his website, allowing viewers to vote for the "hotter" of two randomly chosen photos or rate the looks of students in a particular House against fellow-residents.

A link to the site was forwarded on many House and student group e-mail lists over the weekend—including the Institute of Politics (IOP), Fuerza Latina and the Association of Black Harvard Women (ABHW)—prompting both praise and criticism across campus.

But by Sunday night, outrage from individuals and student groups led Zuckerberg, who said he never expected such widespread publicity, to shut down the site for good[3].

By that time, Zuckerberg said, there had been 450 visitors to the site who had voted on their peers' photos at least 22,000 times.

"I don't see how it can go back online. Issues about violating people's privacy don't seem to be surmountable. The primary concern is hurting people's feelings," Zuckerberg said. "I'm not willing to risk insulting anyone."

Leyla R. Bravo '05, president of Fuerza Latina, said she sent a link to the website out over the group's e-mail list to let people know about what she viewed as a problem.

"I heard from a friend and I was kind of outraged," she said. "I thought people should be aware."

Both Fuerza Latina and ABHW received apology e-mails from Zuckerberg yesterday.

In the letter, Zuckerberg wrote that he was mainly interested in the computer science behind the venture.

"I understood that some parts were still a little sketchy[4] and I wanted some more time to think about whether or not this was really appropriate to release to the Harvard community," he wrote.

According to Zuckerberg, it was his intention to only show a few friends to get their opinion on the site, but someone forwarded the link to a friend and the chain of e-mails continued from there.

"When I returned from a meeting at around 10 p.m.," he wrote in the letter, "traffic was out of hand, and after thinking about the best course of action, I shut down the site around 10:30."

[1] **facebook** = Studenten-Jahrbuch
[2] **concentrator** = a student specializing in a field of study
[3] **for good** = permanently
[4] **sketchy** = not detailed or complete

Skills
How to write creatively p. 86–87

B12 Imagine a girl/the boyfriend of a girl whose photo has been used on Facemash meets Mark Zuckerberg in a hallway. Write a dialogue in which the different views on the programme are expressed.

Getting to the point

Comprehension

C1 Watch extract 3 (20.45 min–23.22 min) and outline what happens in the scene.

DVD

Analysis

C2 Analyze how filmic devices are used to reveal the relationship between the characters involved.

Skills
How to write a text analysis p. 83

Comment

C3 As Zuckerberg was elected "Person of the Year" 2010, TIME devoted a long article to the man and his career. Compare the description of the Zuckerberg in the film as opposed to the Zuckerberg described in the extract from the article below. Judging on the basis of what you have learned about him in this theme discuss which version you would agree with.

Skills
How to write a comment p. 84–85

[...] Zuckerberg's life at Harvard and after was the subject of a movie released in October called *The Social Network* [...]. [It] is a rich, dramatic portrait of a furious, socially handicapped genius who spits corrosive monologues in a monotone to hide his inner pain. This character bears almost no resemblance to the actual Mark Zuckerberg. [...]
Zuckerberg has often – possibly always – been described as remote and socially akward, but that's not quite right. [...] Zuckerberg is a warm presence, not a cold one. He has a quick smile and doesn't shy away from eye contact. He thinks fast and talks fast, but he wants you to keep up. He exudes not anger or social anxiety, but a weird calm. [...]
(TIME, by Lev Grossmann, 1/3/2011)

6 Identity

Getting started

A1 Think about the different aspects of identity reflected in the pictures. Find a suitable heading for each of them.

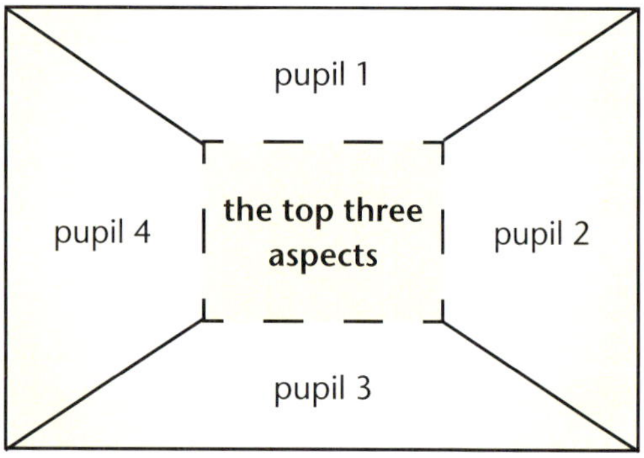

A2 In groups of four work with a placemat:

a) Write down three aspects of identity which are most important for you and explain your choice. You can use ideas from the pictures or your own.

b) Rotate the placemat and write down your comments on the ideas of the others.

c) Finally discuss your ideas in the group and agree on the group's top three aspects.

1

2

3

4

5

6

7

8

9

10

A3 a) Read the quotations on *identity* below. In pairs work on one quotation and explain its meaning in your own words.

b) Present your explanations to the class.

1. "The identity of one changes with how one perceives reality." *(Vithu Jeyaloganathan, Canadian composer, *1991)*

2. "I think history is inextricably linked to identity. If you don't know your history, if you don't know your family, who are you?" *(Mary Pipher, US clinical anthropologist, *1947)*

3. "Work is an essential part of being alive. Your work is your identity. It tells you who you are." *(Kay Stepkin, US baker, *1942)*

4. "Your identity and your success go hand in hand. Many people sacrifice their identities by not doing what they really want to do. And that's why they're not successful." *(Lila Swell, professor of education, Columbia University, *1964)*

5. "An identity would seem to be arrived at by the way in which the person faces and uses his experience." *(James Baldwin, US writer, 1924–1987)*

6. "A racial community provides not only a sense of identity, that luxury of looking into another's face and seeing yourself reflected back, but a sense of security and support." *(Wentworth Miller, US actor, *1972)*

7. "A wife should no more take her husband's name than he should hers. My name is my identity and must not be lost." *(Lucy Stone, US abolitionist and suffragist, 1818–1893)*

A4 With a partner discuss which statements you would agree with most and least.

Practice section

Pre-reading

B1 The central character of the novel "I am the messenger" by Markus Zusak is Ed, who is 19. What would you like to have achieved by the time you are 19?

Comprehension: Analyzing characters

B2 a) Read the extract from Zusak's novel. Describe your first impression of Ed and outline his present situation.

b) Explain which of the quotations from A3 on page 57 fits Ed best.

Sex should be like math: an introduction to my life

I'll tell you a bit about my life.

I play cards at least a few nights a week.

It's what we do.

We play a game called Annoyance, which isn't particularly hard and is the only game we all enjoy without arguing too much.

There's Marv, who never shuts up, sitting there trying to smoke cigars and simultaneously enjoy it.

There's Ritchie, who's always quiet, sporting[1] his laughable tattoo on his right arm. He sips on his longneck beer from start to finish and touches the whiskers[2] that seem glued in patches on his man-boyish face.

There's Audrey. Audrey always sits opposite me, no matter where we play. She has yellow hair, wiry legs, the most beautiful crooked smile in the world, and lovely hips, and she watches a lot of movies. She also works as a cabdriver.

Then there's me.

Before I even mention me, I should tell you some other facts:

1. At nineteen, Bob Dylan was a seasoned[3] performer in Greenwich Village, New York.
2. Salvador Dalí had already produced several outstanding artworks of paint and rebellion by the time he was nineteen.
3. Joan of Arc was the most wanted woman in the world at nineteen, having created a revolution.

Then there's Ed Kennedy, also nineteen ...

Just prior to the bank holdup[4], I'd been taking stock[5] of my life.

Cabdriver – and I'd funked[6] my age at that. (You need to be twenty.)

No real career.

No respect in the community.

Nothing.

I'd realized there were people everywhere achieving greatness while I was taking directions from balding businessmen called Derek and being wary of Friday-night drunks who might throw up in my cab or do a runner on me[7]. It was actually Audrey's idea to give cab driving a shot[8]. It didn't take much to convince me, mainly because I'd been in love with her for years. I never left this suburban town. I didn't go to university. I went to Audrey.

Constantly, I'm asking myself, *Well, Ed – what have you already achieved in your nineteen years?*

The answer's simple.

Jack shit[9].

I mentioned it to a few different people, but all they did was tell me to pull my head in. Marv called me a first-class whinger[10]. Audrey told me I was twenty years too early for a midlife crisis. Ritchie simply looked at me as if I was speaking in a foreign tongue. And when I mentioned it to my ma, she said, "Ohhh, why don't you have a bloody cry, Ed." You're going to love my ma. Trust me.

[1] **to sport sth.** = to display sth., to show so./sth. off
[2] **whiskers** = the hair on a man's cheeks and chin
[3] **seasoned** = *here:* experienced
[4] **bank holdup** = bank robbery; at the beginning of the novel Ed witnesses a bank robbery.
[5] **to take stock of sth.** = to spend some time thinking about the situation you are in before you decide what to do next
[6] **to funk sth.** *(infml)* = to cheat about sth.
[7] **to do a runner on so.** *(infml)* = *here:* to run away from so. (without paying)
[8] **to give sth. a shot** *(infml)* = to try sth.
[9] **jack shit** *(vulg. sl.)* = a small or worthless amount
[10] **whinger** *(Brit. infml)* = so. who complains in an annoying and persistent manner

I live in a shack that I rent cheaply. Not long after moving in, I found out from the real estate agent that my boss was the owner. My boss is the proud founder and director of the cab company I drive for: Vacant Taxis. It's a dubious company, to say the least. Audrey and I had no trouble convincing them that we were old enough and licensed enough to drive for them. Mix a few numbers up on your birth certificate, show up with what appears to be the appropriate license, and you're set. We were driving within a week because they were short-staffed[11]. No reference checks. No fuss[12]. It's surprising what you can achieve with trickery and deceit. As Raskolnikov[13] once said: "When reason fails, the devil helps!" If nothing else, I can lay claim to the title of Youngest Cabdriver in these parts – a taxi-driving prodigy[14]. That's the kind of anti-achievement that gives structure to my life. Audrey's a few months older than me.

The shack I live in is pretty close to town, and since I'm not allowed to take the cab home, it's good walking distance to work. Unless Marv gives me a lift[15]. The reason I don't have a car myself is that I drive people around all day or night. In my time off, the last thing I feel like doing is more driving.

The town we all live in is pretty run-of-the mill[16]. It's past the outskirts of the city and has good and bad parts. I'm sure it won't surprise you that I come from one of the bad parts. My whole family grew up at the far north part of the town, which is kind of like everyone's dirty secret. There are plenty of teenage pregnancies there, a plethora[17] of shithead[18] fathers who are unemployed, and mothers like mine who smoke, drink, and go out in public wearing Ugg boots[19]. The home I grew up in was an absolute dump[20], but I stuck around until my brother, Tommy, finished school and got into university. At times I know I could have done the same, but I was too lazy at school. I was always reading books when I should have been doing math and the rest of it. Maybe I could have got a trade, but they don't give apprenticeships out down there, especially to the likes of me. Due to my aforementioned laziness I was no good at school, except at English, because of the reading. Since my father drank all our money away, I just went straight into work when school was done. I started out in a forgettable hamburger chain that I don't mention, due to shame. Next was sorting files in a dusty accountant's office that closed down within weeks of my arrival. And finally, the height, the pinnacle[21] of my employment history so far.

Cab driving.

[...]

I cook.

I eat.

I wash but I rarely iron.

I live in the past and believe that Cindy Crawford is by far the best supermodel.

That's my life.

I have dark hair, half-tanned skin, coffee brown eyes. My muscles are hugely normal. I should stand straighter, but I don't. I stand with my hands in my pockets. My boots are falling apart, but I still wear them because I love and cherish them.

Quite often, I pull my boots on and go out. Sometimes I go to the river that runs through town, or I go for a walk to the cemetery to see my father. The Doorman comes with me, of course, if he's awake.

What I like best is walking with my hands in my pockets, having the Doorman next to me, and imagining that Audrey's on my other side.

I always picture us from behind.

There's glow turning to darkness.

There's Audrey.

There's the Doorman.

There's me.

And I'm holding Audrey's fingers in mine.

I haven't written a song of Dylan proportions[22] yet, or started painting my first attempt at surrealism, and I doubt I could start a revolution if I tried – because apart from everything else, I'm a bit of an unfit bastard, though I'm lanky and lean. Just weak, too. [...]

[11] **short-staffed** = having fewer people working there than would be desirable
[12] **fuss** = unnecessary worry/excitement about sth.
[13] **Rodion Romanovitch Raskolnikov** = main character in F. Dostoyevski's "Crime and Punishment"
[14] **prodigy** = *here:* a person with exceptional talents or powers
[15] **to give so. a lift** = to drive so. somewhere
[16] **run-of-the-mill** = nullachtfünfzehn
[17] **plethora** = a greater amount than you need or want
[18] **shithead** *(taboo sl.)* = a fool; idiot; used as a term of abuse
[19] **Ugg boots** = fashion boots made of sheepskin
[20] **dump** *(infml)* = a dirty and unpleasant place
[21] **pinnacle** = *here:* the highest point
[22] **proportions** *(pl.)* = *here:* the degree of importance of sth.

Analysis

B3 a) Imagine you want to describe someone interesting to a friend. Write down in keywords what you would talk about.

b) Compare your results with a partner and find categories for describing someone.

B4 Ed is a fictional construct in a novel, not a real person. He serves a certain purpose within the novel. To understand him better you must have a closer look at the text and consider certain features of his character. In the following grid you will find either a definition for a certain aspect or an example from the extract. Write down the missing information.

aspect and definition/explanation	example
1.	2. "I have dark hair, half-tanned skin, coffee brown eyes. My muscles are hugely normal." (ll. 126–127)
3. Personality/Character traits Characters in a novel, as well as real-life people, have unique attributes describing their personality, e.g. (in)tolerance, openness, (dis)honesty etc.	4.
5.	6. "I play cards at least a few nights a week." (l. 2) "I cook. I eat. I wash but I rarely iron." (ll. 120–122)
7. Mood This describes the emotional state a person or character in a novel is in, e.g. (un)happiness.	8.
9. Language/Idiolect This refers to the way a character in a novel talks, uses grammar, vocabulary and pronounces words, which provides information about social background, education and attitudes etc.	10.
11.	12. "The town we all live in [...] has good and bad parts. I'm sure it won't surprise you that I come from one of the bad parts. My whole family grew up at the far north part of the town [...] There are plenty of teenage pregnancies there, a plethora of shithead fathers who are unemployed, and mothers like mine who smoke, drink and go out in public wearing Ugg boots." (ll. 89–98)
13. Relations to others This describes the social relations the character has with others – how does he/she interact with others, how do others interact with him/her and see him/her?	14.
15. Function for the story It is important to look at the function a character has for the story he/she is part of – is he/she the protagonist, a main or a minor character, is he/she the narrator etc.?	16.

Info: Types of character and characterization

In a novel you will find different types of character:

round character	flat character
• dynamic character	• static character
• complex • develops throughout the novel • unpredictable	• simple • does not change • predictable

A character in a fictional text may be presented in different ways:

Telling technique: direct characterization	Showing technique: indirect (dramatic) characterization
The author tells the reader directly and explicitly about the character's looks, traits, attitudes. This can be done by the narrator, the character himself/herself or other characters. Examples: "She has yellow hair, wiry legs, the most beautiful crooked smile in the world [...]." (ll. 16–18) "I was too lazy at school." (ll. 102–103) However, this information may not always be reliable. Since the statements represent the views of different characters, they need not be entirely true, they may be influenced positively by love, or negatively by feelings like jealousy or envy.	You learn a lot about a character by studying what he/she says and does, how he/she behaves in certain situations and interacts with others. The reader is invited to infer traits from the character's action, clothing and body language; he/she must find out for himself/herself. Examples: "Audrey always sits opposite me, no matter where we play." (ll. 15–16) → She seems to be interested in Ed, wants to see his face. "It was actually Audrey's idea to give cab driving a shot." (ll. 43–45) → She is helpful, practical and considerate as she helps Ed organize his life.

B5 a) Look at the highlighted passages in the extract from "I am the messenger" below. In the green parts Ed characterizes himself directly. Note down what you find out about him here.
b) The blue passages contain indirect characterization. Take notes about the kind of person Ed presents himself as here.

[...] Before I even mention me, I should tell you some other facts:
1. At nineteen, Bob Dylan was a seasoned performer in Greenwich Village, New York.
2. Salvador Dali had already produced several outstanding artworks of paint and rebellion by the time he was nineteen.
3. Joan of Arc was the most wanted woman in the world at nineteen, having created a revolution.

Then there's Ed Kennedy, also nineteen ...
Just prior to the bank holdup, I'd been taking stock of my life.
Cabdriver – and I'd funked my age at that. (You need to be twenty.)
No real career. No respect in the community.
Nothing. (ll. 21–38)

B6 Analyze the remaining text to find out more about Ed. Collect information from the text in a grid. For your grid use the categories from B4 on page 60.

category	*direct / explicit*	*indirect / implicit*	*interpretation*
...			
personality/traits		*"I'd funked my age" [to get a cabdriver's license.] (l. 34)*	*Ed is dishonest if necessary or for a practical purpose.*
		"I go for a walk to the cemetery to see my father." (ll. 134–135)	*Ed seems to be sentimental about his father's memory; special relationship son-father*
...			

Skills
How to quote
p. 93

Skills
How to structure a text
p. 98

B7 Use your results from B4 to B6 to write a detailed characterization of Ed as a character in the novel. Remember to provide evidence for your findings by referring to and quoting from the text.

Follow these steps to plan and write your characterization:

1. **Introduction:** State who you are writing about and what the focus of your analysis will be.

2. **Main part:** Use the categories of characterization to organize the main part in a topical order. This is preferable to a chronological order as working through the text chronologically often produces unnecessary repetitions.

3. **Conclusion:** At the end, summarize your results in an abstract, general way.

Language support: characterization

introduction	**main part**	**conclusion**
• Ed, the protagonist of the novel, appears to be an ambivalent character. • Ed, the first-person narrator of the novel, describes his life and circumstances and reveals that he is lost/doesn't know what to do with his life.	• The character is presented/ described as .../in a ... way. • His body language reveals/ suggests ... • When he claims that/ comments on/protests that ..., it becomes obvious that ... • The fact that he ... (action) reveals/highlights/ underlines that ...	• As a result of the analysis, Ed can be described as ... • The detailed characterization proves that ... but at the same time ... • The essential outcome of my analysis is that Ed is actually ...

Creative writing

B8 Choose a task:

- Audrey is Ed's best friend and his love. But she just wants him to be her friend and not her boyfriend. She is a kind, caring, thoughtful, and gentle person.
  Audrey feels that Ed is not happy with his life. After one of their evenings of playing cards she confronts him and tries to motivate him to do something. Write their dialogue. Try to imitate the way Ed talks.

Or:

- Ed's brother Tommy calls. He is enthusiastic about his life at university and enquires about Ed's life and perspectives. Write their telephone dialogue. Make sure you imitate the way Ed talks.

Skills
How to write creatively p. 86–87

Checklist

✓ Any creative writing task you will be given in your exam will require that the fictional text you produce is based on what you have previously found out about the original text.

What have you found out from the original text?

Content: Stick to the plot as it has developed up to this point.

✓ What has happened so far?
✓ What do you know about the character/s?
✓ How do they feel about the current problem?
✓ What mood are the characters in?
→ What might the characters' plans/intentions be? How might they react?

Language: Adopt an appropriate register.

✓ How does the character speak?
→ Depending on the point of view of your character, use an appropriate idiolect (register, sentence structure, choice of words).
✓ What is typical of the author's style?

- Is the choice of words simple, sophisticated, scientific?
- Are the sentences simple or complex?
- Is the focus on narrative passages or on dialogue?
- Does the author use imagery in his/her descriptions?
- Try to imitate these aspects in your text production.

Language support: dialogue

When you write a *dialogue,* remember to use typical features of spoken language like

- elliptical sentences, especially in questions/exclamations: "What? He wouldn't. Never."
- question tags: "He's never understood me, has he?"
- hesitation devices: "Well, ...", "Basically ...", "Actually ...", "You know ..."
- colloquial language (if appropriate for the speakers involved and the given situation): "I'm gonna ...", "He ain't ..."
- contact clauses: "She is the girl I have been looking for."

These features apply to dialogues in a prose text, plays or film scripts. They can also be used in a diary entry, an interior monologue or even in an informal letter since these forms imitate spoken language.

Getting to the point

Pre-reading

C1 Growing up in a multicultural environment is not always easy, as you may be confronted with different cultural backgrounds, different habits and customs, or different value systems.
The first person narrator of the novel "(Un)arranged marriage" by Bali Rai is a teenage boy, Manjit, from a traditional Punjabi family who lives in Leicester in the East Midlands of England. Think-pair-share: speculate about the problems he may encounter in the family.

Comprehension

C2 Read the extract from the novel and describe Manjit's situation in his family in your own words. Consider the different members of his family and how their behaviour affects Manjit's life.

Analysis: characterization

Skills
How to write a text analysis p. 83

C3 Write a characterization of Manjit. Consider the author's use of direct and indirect characterization. Assess the extent to which Manjit is presented as a round character. Before you start writing collect information from the text in a grid like in B6.

Creative writing

Skills
How to write creatively p. 86–87

C4 Ranjit, Manjit's older brother, can see that Manjit will not turn into "a newer version" of their father like himself. Talking to a Punjabi friend he complains about Manjit and comments on his father's reaction. Write their dialogue.

Extract from "(Un)arranged marriage" by Bali Rai

[...] And my dad, well, he ran the family with fear. He was always either at work or sitting around, pissed[1] on Teacher's whisky, shouting at everyone. He got angry all the time, maybe at something he'd seen on the TV or some problem at work, or sometimes for no reason at all. I'd never seen him hit my mum or anything like that. With her and my sister-in-law he just shouted a lot which scared them enough anyway. I had seen him hit my brothers though, whenever they were out of order[2], which was not that often because they were basically turning into newer versions of him and that was what he wanted all his sons to be.

With me though it was like open season[3]. He'd hit me for asking him too many questions or for daring to say something back to him. One time, he'd clipped me round the head for having a go at Harry, and I had answered back calling him a "bastard". I got beaten that day with his old hockey stick that he kept under the stairs and I had to tell everyone at school that I had hurt myself playing football. He hit me all the

[1] **to be pissed** *(sl)* = to be drunk
[2] **out of order** = behaviour that is out of order is annoying because it is not suitable for a particular situation
[3] **open season** = the period during which it is legal to hunt; *(infml)* a time of unrestrained harassment, criticism, or attack

time, sometimes I reckon just because I was in his range. It was either his fists or his feet or anything hard that came to hand. Not that I was that bothered by it. I mean, he'd been doing it since I was a kid and I just saw it as one of the daily hazards of growing up – trying to avoid getting hit. I did wonder though why he singled me out. Sometimes I thought it was because I was the youngest and other times I really thought that he hated me for some reason, only I was never told what it was. Maybe he could see that I was more influenced by the whole Western culture thing than my brothers had been. He definitely didn't like the fact that my best friend wasn't Asian. Either way, getting hit all the time made me feel an outsider and the feeling just got stronger as I grew older.

We lived on Evington Drive, in an area that was popular with Punjabi families. There were only three bedrooms which meant that I had to move out of my box room and in with Harry when Ranjit got married and his wife moved in with us. Ranjit and Jas got my old room, even though it only just had room for their bed, but that was their problem. They were the ones who had nicked[4] my room from me.

Sharing a room with Harry was like my worst nightmare. He was fat and hairy, and had a horrible habit of leaving his dirty football kit, muddy boots included, all over the place. He only bathed every three days and in the summer the room stank of stale sweat when he'd been lifting weights. At night I used to pretend that he wasn't there by pulling the duvet over myself like a tent and reading by torchlight. Even then he'd throw things at me or call me a poof[5].

"What you wanna read for, man? Bloody Dickens – what are you, a gorah (white) or something? Read about bloody man's stuff, innit[6]."

I hated having no privacy, no time to myself that wasn't intruded on by a brother who still found fart jokes incredibly funny. He was so bloody thick[7], it was like talking to a gorilla sometimes. I hated him. And he'd turn up like a bad smell every time I wanted some peace, no matter where I was – the garden, the garage, wherever. Recently Ranjit and his wife had started doing the same, always around and giggling at each other like kids.

My mum was always in the kitchen, cooking, or watching the Asian channels on Sky in the living room. And Dad? Well, he was a law unto himself, walking around the house like a drunken zombie, belching all the time. To escape, I'd tried locking myself in the bathroom once but only succeeded in getting a smack in the mouth from him for my trouble. I couldn't even do my homework in peace because no-one in my family saw it as being important. They thought that school was a waste of time, like quite a lot of working-class Punjabi families. All they were interested in was trying to earn money and you couldn't do that at school or college. Ranjit and Harry had both got jobs in factories as soon as they left school. It was a wonder that I ever got the high grades that I did – not that anyone in my family cared. [...]

[4] **to nick** *(infml)* = to steal
[5] **poof** *(offensive sl)* = a homosexual male
[6] **innit** *(infml)* = used as a general question tag after any statement, especially by young British Asians
[7] **thick** *(infml)* = *here:* stupid

7 Multiculturalism

Getting started

A1 a) Associations: Write down three words that immediately come to your mind when you think of the word *multiculturalism*.

b) Compare your associations with your partner's.

c) Study the poster and the two quotations and describe what they say about multiculturalism in your own words.

d) Compare them with your own ideas and identify common features with regard to the topic multiculturalism.

[1] **melting pot** = Immigrants of different cultures or races form an integrated society
[2] **strand** = *here*: one part of American society

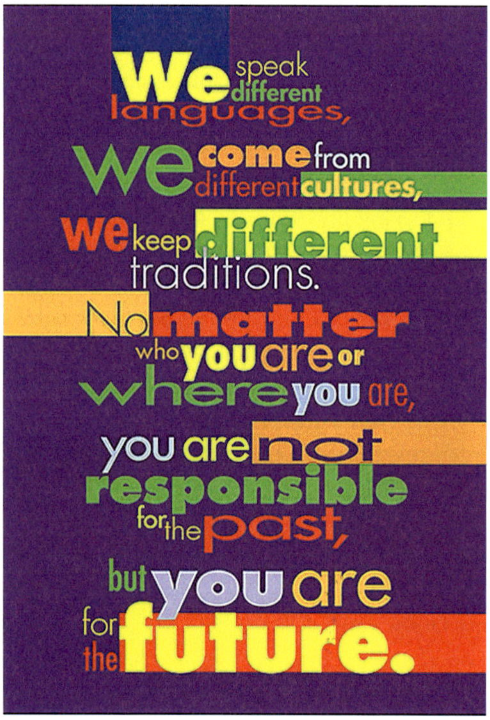

"We become not a melting pot[1] but a beautiful mosaic. Different people, different beliefs, different yearnings, different hopes, different dreams."
*Jimmy Carter (*1924)*
39th president of the USA, 1977–1981

"Fortunately, the time has long passed when people liked to regard the United States as some kind of melting pot, taking men and women from every part of the world and converting them into standardized, homogenized Americans. We are, I think, much more mature and wise today. Just as we welcome a world of diversity, so we glory in an America of diversity – an America all the richer for the many different and distinctive strands[2] of which it is woven."
Hubert Humphrey (1911–1978),
vice president of the USA, 1965–1969

Language support
to persuade so.
to influence so.
to assure so.
to talk so. into sth.
to convince so.
to win so. over
to manipulate so.
to achieve one's aim
to hammer home one's point/ message

A2 a) Read the following extracts from famous speeches about multiculturalism and say how they make you feel.

b) Talk to your partner about how these feelings are evoked.

c) Identify the speakers' points of view on multiculturalism and compare them with your results from A1c) and d).

d) Study the photos and speculate on what the gestures and facial expressions indicate about the speakers' intentions. Use some of the words from the language support.

e) Exchange ideas with a partner.

"It's just like when you've got some coffee that's too black, which means it's too strong. What do you do? You integrate it with cream, you make it weak. But if you pour too much cream in it, you won't even know you ever had coffee. It used to be hot, it becomes cool. It used to be strong, it becomes weak. It used to wake you up, now it puts you to sleep."
Malcolm X

"It was whispered by slaves and abolitionists as they blazed a trail toward freedom[1] through the darkest of nights.
Yes we can.
It was sung by immigrants as they struck out from distant shores and pioneers who pushed westward against an unforgiving wilderness.
Yes we can.
It was the call of workers who organized; women who reached for the ballot; a president who chose the moon as our new frontier; and a King who took us to the mountaintop and pointed the way to the Promised Land.
Yes we can to justice and equality. Yes we can to opportunity and prosperity.
Yes we can heal this nation. Yes we can repair this world. Yes we can."
Barack Obama, US president since January 2009

[1] **to blaze a trail toward freedom** = to begin the fight for freedom

"I have a dream that one day on the red hills of Georgia the sons of former slaves and the sons of former slave-owners will be able to sit down together at a table of brotherhood.
I have a dream that one day even the state of Mississippi, a desert state, sweltering with the heat of injustice and oppression, will be transformed into an oasis of freedom and justice.
I have a dream that my four children will one day live in a nation where they will not be judged by the colour of their skin but by the content of their character.
I have a dream today."
"I Have a Dream" speech by Martin Luther King, August 28th, 1963

Practice section

Pre-reading

DVD

B1 a) Listen to the speech by Peter Sellers and say what he is actually talking about.

b) Listen to the speech again while reading the text. Check whether your ideas from a) were correct.

c) Explain what makes this speech funny and what Peter Sellers' intentions might have been.

d) Copy words and phrases from the text that you consider useful when delivering a speech.

Language support
satire /ˈsætaɪə/
satirical /səˈtɪrɪkl/
irony /ˈaɪrəni/
ironic /aɪˈrɒnɪk/
humorous
comic effect
comedy

Tip
You can only deliver a speech, give a speech or make a speech. But you cannot hold a speech!

Peter Sellers: Party Political Speech

My friends, in the light of present-day developments let me say right away that I do not regard existing conditions likely. On the contrary, I have always regarded them as subjects of the gravest responsibility and shall ever continue to do so. Indeed, I will even go further and state quite categorically that I am more than sensible of the definition of the precise issues which are at this very moment concerning us all. We must build, but we must build surely. [Hear, hear!] Let me say just this: If any part of what I am saying is challenged, then I am more than ready to meet such a challenge. For I have no doubt whatsoever that whatever I may have said in the past, or what I am saying now, is the exact, literal and absolute truth as to the state of the case. [Hear, hear!] I put it to you that this is not the time for vague promises of better things to come. For, if I were to convey to you a spirit of false optimism, then I should be neither fair to you nor true to myself. But does this mean, I hear you cry, that we can no longer look forward to the future that is to come? Certainly not! [What about the workers?] "What about the workers?" indeed sir! Grasp, I beseech you, with both hands [Aside: I'm so sorry, I beg your pardon, madam.] the opportunities that are offered. Let us assume a bold front and go forward together. Let us carry the fight against ignorance to the four corners of the earth because it is a fight which concerns us all. Now, finally my friends, in conclusion, let me say just this: ...

Comprehension

Skills
How to write a summary p. 82

B2 a) Read the speech "Happy Australia Day" given by the Australian MP Peter Debnam in 2007 and identify the speaker's message.

b) Summarize the main points of Debnam's argument.

Peter Debnam's Australia Day Speech: Happy Australia Day!

On days like today you reflect on the extraordinary achievement of what Australia has become. We are a truly unique and special people, no matter where we have come from.

There is a substance to the character of our community, based on Australian values and culture that have been built up over generations. Volunteering, community service, respect for others, personal responsibility have all taken pride of place.

English is and always will be our first and unifying language. However, we also embrace[1] the second languages of the many different backgrounds of Australians as community assets[2], especially in the pursuit of understanding and friendships with our international neighbours.

And we live in a pristine natural environment that enables us to enjoy the greatest lifestyle you could hope for.

In Australia we work to live, not the other way around. We value the time we really share with our family and friends, especially on days like today. And as a community we have much to celebrate.

As citizens we can never take for granted our lifestyle, our environment and the friendly and open nature that Australians are famous for.

These privileges carry great responsibilities, especially for political leaders, to ensure they are protected, preserved and promoted.

Over the years […] I have become increasingly concerned, however, at how political correctness has hijacked[3] and marginalized[4] multiculturalism in Australia, driving wedges[5] into our community, rather than bringing Australians together.

Today I want to reclaim multiculturalism for mainstream Australians who believe that it should be a policy for inclusion, not exclusion.

No longer can we allow multiculturalism to justify the barriers placed between Australians of different backgrounds, different faiths and different beliefs. It must become a rallying point[6] to live as an inclusive society, living a uniquely Australian way of life.

Multiculturalism must be a policy for integration not separation. It must be a policy that shows respect for our different cultural backgrounds, including indigenous Australians, but a policy that focuses on Australian values and an Australian way of life that we share as a first priority.

After all it was these same values and the opportunity for an Australian way of life that has attracted millions of new Australians to our shores for centuries.

The apologists for political correctness equate importation of nationalist and religious rivalries with the timeless values of centuries old cultures. It's just nonsense.

Australians are fed up with seeing the problems of other nations played out on our own streets, our own sporting venues, our own beaches and even in our own schools. Even this year's Australian Open could not escape these rivalries. And when they start rioting at the tennis, you know you've got a problem.

The politically correct and extreme agenda for multiculturalism in Australia poses a very serious threat to the openness and inclusive nature of our society.

Becoming an Australian citizen does not give you the right to a patch of land, where you simply recreate your old country in the new – separated from the rest of the community. It's the entitlement to embrace and participate in a new Australian way of life.

Under no circumstances can we give a green light to cultural segregation in our community. […]

All Australians need to see themselves as Australians. And all Australians need to accept each other as Australians. We cannot allow ourselves to invest our identity only in our differences.

By allowing communities within our society to overtly differentiate themselves in this way and fail to embrace a common Australia, we light the fuse[7] to more conflicts in the future.

Australia is an inclusive society. Australia is a society that you become part of, that you participate in and that you contribute to.

The answer to these problems lies in what Prime Minister John Howard has been talking about for years. We need to get some basic priorities sorted out and put initiatives in place to promote tolerance and to promote acceptance of our

[1] **to embrace sth.** = to enthusiastically accept sth.
[2] **asset** = a benefit
[3] **to hijack sth.** = *here*: political correctness now threatens multiculturalism
[4] **to marginalize** = to make so. or sth. seem not important
[5] **to drive wedges into a community** = to cause problems between people
[6] **rallying point** = a point or principle on which opposing groups can come together
[7] **to light the fuse** = *here*: encourage

differences, but most importantly celebrate what we share as Australians first.

To this end I am announcing a series of measures today as part of my plan to take back multiculturalism for mainstream Australia – what I call *practical multiculturalism*.

To do this I announce that a Debnam Liberal/National's Government in New South Wales will introduce firstly:

• A new Australian Values and Civics Test for year 6 students based on the test recently introduced by the Australian Government for new citizens. We will review the curriculum to ensure it encompasses all the material covered in the new test, especially Australian history, with equal focus on colonial and indigenous history.

• We'll rename the existing *English as a Second Language* Program to become *Teaching English as a First Language* Program and the provision of an additional 200 new teachers to reverse Labor's 12 years of language neglect.

• We'll establish free English Language courses at the same Community Colleges to assist those who wish to develop their English language skills.

• We'll establish a new free Civics and Citizenship course at NSW Community Colleges.

• And importantly, we'll establish a $6 million Youth Community Partnership Projects Program to provide financial assistance for schools and community organisations to arrange and undertake projects that involve young people from different cultural backgrounds, different schools and different areas working together on charitable and other community initiatives.

I believe this package will make a positive contribution to creating a more inclusive society. I believe, as Premier, you need to take a practical leadership role on these issues wherever you can – not just talk about them.

Can I conclude by congratulating all of those who become Australian citizens on this day. I welcome you to your new life as an Australian and look forward to the contribution you will make to our great country.

Happy Australia Day.

Analysis: Rhetorical/Stylistic devices in political speeches

Language support

to evoke
to suggest
to call to one's mind
to imply
to advocate
to convey
to hint at sth.

Skills
How to write a text analysis p. 83

B3 Analyze the rhetorical devices Debnam employs in his Australia Day speech and explain their effects on the audience. In order to do this you should

- study the devices in the info-box on page 71.
- identify and name the rhetorical devices used in the speech.
- explain why he uses them and to what effect.

Example:

1) Debnam uses the rhetorical device of antithesis to underline his argument. By contrasting opposing ideas in one sentence, he stresses the fact that inclusion not exclusion is the right way to achieve a multicultural society, e.g. (ll. 38–40) "Today I want to reclaim multiculturalism for mainstream Australians who believe that it should be a policy for inclusion, not exclusion."

2) Debnam also employs alliteration to emphasize his point of view: (ll. 31–32) "[...] to ensure they are protected, preserved and promoted." At the same time, this is an example of a group of three words, which again underlines his point.

Checklist

✓ State the topic dealt with in the political speech (introduction).
✓ Identify the most obvious and most effectively used rhetorical devices.
✓ Explain their effects.
✓ Explain the interplay of the speaker's message and the means used to convince the audience.
✓ Use appropriate vocabulary (see language support).

Info: Rhetorical devices, definitions and their effects

rhetorical device	definitions and effects
alliteration	emphasis that occurs through the repetition of initial consonant letters of two or more neighbouring words, e.g. "bigger box", "red rose"
allusion	a reference to a famous historical or literary figure or event, e.g. "a King who took us to the mountaintop and pointed the way to the Promised Land" (Obama refers to Martin Luther King, who explained his vision of America's future in his "I Have a Dream" speech)
anaphora	the repetition of identical words in successive phrases or sentences to put emphasis on sth., e.g. "We'll establish free English language courses ... We'll establish a new free Civics and Citizenship course ..."
antithesis/contrast	a contrast between two things; denotes the opposing of ideas by means of grammatically parallel arrangements of words, clauses or sentences so as to produce an effective contrast, e.g. "It used to be hot, it becomes cool. It used to be strong, it becomes weak." (Malcolm X)
exaggeration	representing (something) as being larger, greater, better, or worse than it really is, e.g. "We've heard this complaint a thousand times."
group of three	a group of three related ideas or concepts, e.g. "our openness, our hospitality and our belief"
inversion	the reversal of the normal order of words, typically for rhetorical effect, e.g. "No longer can we believe in the truth of his words."
metaphor	a word or phrase used to describe sb./sth. else which creates an image in the reader's mind and makes the description more powerful, e.g. "they blazed a trail toward freedom through the darkest of nights" (Barack Obama)
parallelism	the same or similar sentence patterns, e.g. "pay any price, bear any burden, support any friend"
receiver-including words or pronouns	directly addressing the audience to create a sense of unity or identity, e.g. "we", "my friends", "fellow countrymen"
repetition	repeating certain words or phrases for the purpose of emphasis, e.g. "different people, different beliefs, different yearnings, different hopes, different dreams" (Jimmy Carter)
rhetorical question	a question which expects no answer, e.g. "Don't we all want to become rich and famous?"

Comment/Creative writing

B4 Assess Debnam's success in conveying his message to the audience.

Skills
How to write a comment p. 84–85

B5 Your school wants to become a racism-free school and has applied to the European Council to be awarded Europe's "racism-free school" logo. Part of the application process is a speech that has to be delivered to the committee which makes the final decision. Write a one-minute speech in which you convince the committee that your school deserves to carry that logo:

- Use some of the phrases you copied from Peter Sellers' speech in B1d).
- Employ some rhetorical devices from the info-box.

Deliver your speech to the class. Practise gestures and facial expressions as well as intonation in advance.

Skills
How to write a speech p. 91

Getting to the point

Comprehension

C1 Read the speech "I have a plan to destroy America" given by Richard D. Lamm in 2004 and identify the speaker's message.

Analysis

Skills
How to write a text analysis p. 83

C2 Analyze Lamm's speech:

a) Examine the argumentative structure of the speech.

b) Identify rhetorical devices and explain their effects on the audience.

Comment

Skills
How to write a comment p. 84–85

C3 Comment on Lamm's plan.

I Have a Plan to Destroy America

I have a secret plan to destroy America. If you believe, as many do, that America is too smug[1], too white bread[2], too self-satisfied, too rich, let's destroy America. It is not that hard to do. History shows that nations are more fragile than their citizens think. […] Here is my plan:

1 We must first make America a bilingual-bicultural country. History shows, in my opinion, that no nation can survive the tension, conflict and antagonism of two competing languages and cultures. It is a blessing for an individual to be bilingual; it is a curse for a society to be bilingual. One scholar, Seymour Martin Lipset, put it this way: "The histories of bilingual and bicultural societies that do not assimilate are histories of turmoil, tension and tragedy. Canada, Belgium, Malaysia, Lebanon – all face crises of national existence in which minorities press for autonomy, if not independence. Pakistan and Cyprus have divided. Nigeria suppressed an ethnic rebellion. France faces difficulties with its Basques, Bretons and Corsicans."

2 I would then invent "multiculturalism" and encourage immigrants to maintain their own culture. I would make it an article of belief that all cultures are equal: that there are no cultural differences that are important. I would declare it an article of faith that the black and Hispanic dropout rate[3] is only due to prejudice and discrimination by the majority. Every other explanation is out-of-bounds[4].

3 We can make the United States a "Hispanic Quebec" without much effort. The key is to

[1] **smug** = to be too pleased about sth. you have done or achieved
[2] **white bread** = *here:* traditional
[3] **dropout rate** = number of people who leave school before they have finished their studies
[4] **out-of-bounds** = *here:* banned, out of the question

celebrate diversity rather than unity. [...] I would encourage all immigrants to keep their own language and culture. I would replace the melting pot metaphor with a salad bowl metaphor. It is important to insure that we have various cultural sub-groups living in America reinforcing their differences, rather than Americans emphasizing their similarities.

4 Having done all this, I would make our fastest-growing demographic group the least educated – I would add a second underclass, unassimilated, undereducated and antagonistic to our population. I would have this second underclass have a 50 percent dropout rate from school.

5 I would then get the big foundations and big business to give these efforts lots of money. I would invest in ethnic identity, and I would establish the cult of victimology[5]. I would get all minorities to think their lack of success was all the fault of the majority. I would start a grievance industry blaming all minority failure on the majority population.

6 I would establish dual citizenship and promote divided loyalties. I would "celebrate diversity." "Diversity" is a wonderfully seductive word. It stresses differences rather than commonalities. Diverse people worldwide are mostly engaged in hating each other – that is, when they are not killing each other. A "diverse," peaceful or stable society is against most historical precedent. People undervalue the unity it takes to keep a nation together, and we can take advantage of this myopia[6]. Look at the ancient Greeks. Dorf's "World History" tells us: "The Greeks believed that they belonged to the same race; they possessed a common language and literature; and they worshipped the same gods. All Greece took part in the Olympic Games in honor of Zeus, and all Greeks venerated the shrine of Apollo at Delphi. A common enemy, Persia, threatened their liberty. Yet, all of these bonds together were not strong enough to overcome two factors ... (local patriotism and geographical conditions that nurtured[7] political divisions ...)." If we can put the emphasis on the "pluribus[8]", instead of the "unum," we can balkanize[9] America as surely as Kosovo.

7 Then I would place all these subjects off-limits – make it taboo to talk about. I would find a word similar to "heretic" in the 16th century – that stopped discussion and paralyzed thinking. Words like "racist", "xenophobe[10]" halt argument and conversation. Having made America a bilingual-bicultural country, having established multiculturalism, having the large foundations fund the doctrine of "victimology," I would next make it impossible to enforce our immigration laws. I would develop a mantra[11] – "because immigration has been good for America, it must always be good." I would make every individual immigrant sympatric[12] and ignore the cumulative impact.

8 Lastly, I would censor Victor Davis Hanson's book "Mexifornia" – this book is dangerous; it exposes my plan to destroy America. So please, please – if you feel that America deserves to be destroyed – please, please – don't buy this book! This guy is on to my plan.

Richard D. Lamm, a Democrat,
served as governor of Colorado for 12 years
from 1975 to 1987.

[5] **victimology** = study of issues to do with victims of crimes
[6] **myopia** = shortsightedness
[7] **to nurture** = *here:* to support the conditions for sth. to grow
[8] **"e pluribus unum"** = (*Latin*) "out of many, one" (a motto of the United States)
[9] **to balkanize** = *here:* to split up or break up a country into regions that are hostile to each other
[10] **xenophobe** = a fear or dislike of people from other countries or cultures
[11] **mantra** = words or phrases that are spoken again and again
[12] **sympatric** = species which exist in the same geographical area without interbreeding

8 Sexual identity

Getting started

A1 a) Study the two photos and tell your partner your immediate reaction.

b) Discuss the significance of the words "but" and "still" in the second picture.

c) Explain the connection between the facial expressions and posture of the three teenagers and the message expressed in the words.

d) In groups of three – one pupil for each person in the photographs – speak the two lines aloud expressing different emotions: anger, fear, boredom, humour and passion.

A2 a) Read the extract from "Citizenship" by Mark Ravenhill quietly first.

b) Divide into five groups: Find a partner within your group. Each group practises reading the lines in a different way. Group 1: angry, group 2: frightened, group 3: bored, group 4: giggly, group 5: passionate

c) One pair from each group presents their version to the class.

d) Discuss the different effects created by your dramatic readings and decide on the most appropriate version.

Extract from "Citizenship" by Mark Ravenhill

[...]

Tom You're alright. You're a good person. I like you.

Amy Yeah?

Tom I really like you.

Amy Thass good.

Tom You got a nice face.

Amy kisses Tom.

Oh.

Amy Was that wrong?

Tom I didn't mean you to do that.

Amy Oh. Right. Right.

Tom I didn't wanna kiss you. Only –

Amy Yeah?

Tom I'm not ready for –

Amy You're fifteen.

Tom I know.

Amy You gotta have done.

Tom No.

Amy Why?

Tom It doesn't matter.

Amy Tell me.

Tom I have this dream. And in this dream I'm kissing someone. Real kissing. Tongues and that. But I can't see who I'm kissing. I don't know if it's a woman. Or a man. I try to see the face. But I can't.

Amy Are you gay?

Tom I don't know.

Amy There's bisexual.

Tom You won't tell anyone?

Amy No. Are you going to decide?

Tom What?

Amy What you are?

Tom I don't know.

Amy Or find out?

Tom I don't know.

Amy Don't waste yourself, Tom. You've got a nice face.

Amy Yeah.

[...]

A3 a) Find a partner who had the same role as you in A2 (Amy or Tom). Go through your character's lines and discuss what the character might actually be thinking while speaking those lines. Write down his or her thoughts.

b) Find another pair who wrote down the thoughts of the other character.

- Amy and Tom should be sitting next to each other while the persons with their "thoughts" could stand behind them.
- Amy and Tom: Read your lines slowly to each other.
- Amy and Tom's thoughts: Read out Amy and Tom's thoughts that go with their spoken lines.

c) In your group discuss to what extent adding the characters' thoughts helps you understand them.

A4 a) Amy and Tom talk about intimate things like their sexual orientation. If you had to stage this particular scene, what kind of setting and scenery would you choose? In groups of four discuss your ideas and come to a decision about:

- setting
- props
- lighting effects
- scenery/stage design
- costumes
- sound effects

Language support

These sentence beginnings can help you express your ideas:

- If I were the director, ...
- If I had to stage the play, ...
- The setting should take into account ...
- The scenery could reflect ...
- I suggest that the costumes ...
- My idea would be to include pauses and silences because ...
- I would choose the following props to underline ...

Language support: drama terms

- cast/dramatist
- playwright/director
- script
- stage directions
- stage design/scenery/props/lighting effects/sound effects/volume
- pauses/silences
- dialogue/monologue
- gestures/facial expressions
- scene
- to stage a play
- to perform a role
- to cast so. in a role

b) Compare your ideas in class.

Practice section

Pre-reading

B1 a) Think-pair-share: in what contexts and in what ways is sexuality or sexual identity a subject you talk about
- at school?
- in private outside school?

b) Explain to what extent the two different settings have an impact on the ways sexuality is discussed.

Comprehension

B2 a) Read the extract from "A Vampire Story" by Moira Buffini.

b) In groups of seven create a freeze frame that visualizes the scene. In order to be able to do that you first have to discuss aspects such as the relationships between the characters or the atmosphere.

c) Present your freeze frames to the other groups. Let the audience first describe who and what they see. Then explain your intentions.

d) Decide which freeze frame best captures the scene.

This Extract from Moira Buffini's play "A Vampire Story" is set during the first drama lesson in the new school year. Mint is the drama teacher. All other characters are his students: Frank, Briggs and Moon are schoolboys; Debit, Point, and Ella/Eleanor are schoolgirls.

Frank has sensitive eyes and a nervous demeanour[1]. Mint is full of fervour[2] and frustration. Mint's students, Briggs, Point, Debit and Moon, have perfected an air of cultivated boredom. They look as if they haven't had any fresh air in years. They look in fact, like detached, fashionable, effortlessly nonchalant vampires.

[...]

Mint So, same old spoilt rebels and fashion victims as last year. Not allowed to swear with disappointment or I would. Briggs

Briggs Mint

Mint I'm gutted[3] to see you; I thought you'd be shovelling fries for the rest of your life. And Debit

Debit Hello, Mint

Mint You actually passed an exam?

Debit Might have

Mint So there's a brain somewhere under all that hair spray

Debit It's mousse

Mint Well, let's see how long you last

Point No, Mint, why don't we see how long you last?

Mint We're off to a great start already. Now, I'm more than delighted to see that we have some new blood. What are your names?

Ella Eleanor Wythenshawe

Mint And?

Frank Frank Adam Stein

Mint OK, Ella and – one name will do – Frank. I'm going to throw you in at the deep end. What's the first rule of making drama? Come on! First rule of making drama?

Debit Just say 'Yes'

Mint Thank you, Debit. 'Yes'. Yes to an idea, yes to each other, yes to the energy, to the communal experience, yes to the mighty, universal 'yes'. That's what we aspire to in this class, isn't it?

Moon No

Mint So. The hot seat[4]. Frank – let's start with you

Frank What?

[1] **demeanour** = the way a person behaves towards others
[2] **fervour** = very strong feeling or enthusiasm
[3] **to be gutted** = to be disappointed
[4] **hot seat** = the person in role is questioned or interviewed by other students and answers questions as that character.

Mint takes Frank to a seat apart from the group.

Mint We're going to put you on the hot seat

Frank What for? Why?

Briggs To scald[5] your arse

Mint The hot seat, guys, is a place of discovery, OK? Now we usually use it when we're 'in character', but I'm going to do something we've never tried before. I'm an instinctive teacher and my instincts are saying, 'Go, Mint, go.' So I'm going to throw away the code of good practice and hot seat you as yourself

Moon That's psychological torture, Mint

Mint It's going to be fun, OK?

Moon You could leave him permanently scarred

Mint Frank, the rest of the group will ask you questions

Moon You're infringing his human rights

Mint And your only job is to be truthful

Moon These are torture chamber conditions

Mint It's a simple question and answer exercise. Are you being tortured, Frank?

Frank Um

Mint Now, think about everything that has brought you to this moment in time. People, when I clap my hands we're going to begin – so have your questions for Frank ready

Frank is full of dread. Mint claps.

Moon Do you feel that in doing this, Mint is infringing your human rights?

Frank Um

Briggs What's your name?

Frank I've already said it

Briggs I didn't listen

Frank Frank

Briggs Frank what?

Frank Stein

Briggs What's that short for?

Frank Franklin

Moon Your name's Franklinstein?

Briggs *(laughing)* Are you lying?

Frank My dad thought it was funny too. In fact, it was his last big joke before his sense of humour calcified[6] and had to be removed

Point Are you a monster?

Frank Probably

Briggs Are you a wanker[7]?

Mint Briggs!

Debit What school were you at before, Franklin?

Frank I'm home-educated

Debit What?

Frank My mum and dad have been teaching me at home

Briggs How long for?

Frank Since I was a foetus

Moon You've never been to school?

Frank No

Point Why not?

Frank You'll have to ask my parents that really

Point No thanks

Frank Perhaps they were worried that I might grow up normal if I went to school so they decided to concentrate all their efforts on turning me into a freak

Point Why?

Frank Well, they're freaks, so I expect they just wanted me to fit in

Mint Frank, I can understand your defensiveness, but just try to be open. Say yes

Frank Well, to be fair on my mum and dad – that's Tina and Geoff – I think they had high hopes. They wanted me to fulfil my potential

Point What potential is that, Franklin?

Frank Tina and Geoff thought that if I learnt everything there is to know by the age of sixteen I might turn out to be a leader of men or a genius or something but I eventually had to point out the flaw in their plan and say, 'Tina and Geoff, if you don't let me go to school and talk to some other people, I'll end up in a nut house[8] before I'm twenty,' and to drive home[9] my point I painted my bedroom black and drowned Tina's pot plants so, given that I've got four 'A's at A Level already, they decided to let me come. They see it as a bit of a gap year, I think

Moon Did you say you were a genius?

Frank No, I'm a great disappointment

Briggs Are you gay?

Mint Question not allowed

Moon Is God a man or a woman?

Frank Pardon?

Mint I think he means are you religious?

Moon No, is God a man or a woman?

Frank Um, if there was a deity or creator I'd say it would be unlikely to have recognisable genitalia

[5] **to scald** = to burn with hot liquid or steam
[6] **to calcify** = to become hard, inflexible or unchanging
[7] **wanker** *(offensive sl)* = a stupid or unpleasant person; so. who masturbates
[8] **nut house** = an institution for the mentally ill
[9] **to drive home** = make clear by special emphasis and try to convince so. of sth.

Debit That's rude

Frank God probably transcends gender. The deity is probably asexual or even polysexual

Point Is that what you are, Frank?

Frank It may even be formless, dare I say it, non-existent and therefore imaginable in any form

Debit I think you're shy about sex

Frank Is that a question?

Debit That's cute. You got any diseases?

Mint Not allowed

Debit Have you got a girlfriend, Frank?

Frank No

Briggs Have you got any friends at all?

Frank Yes, no, well, it depends what you mean by friends. If you mean actual living people who like me, then no

Debit That's a bit sad, isn't it?

Frank I used to have an imaginary friend, but he moved out. He was great; really funny; much more daring than me. He used to subvert Geoff's quizzes and put lighted matches in the bin, but in the end he had to go

Moon Why?

Frank It turned out he was hiding pornography under the bed and Tina found it. She had a massive row with him. He came in to tell me he was leaving and I haven't seen him since

Ella Do you miss him?

Frank Yes

Debit So what d'you do for fun, Frank?

Frank Fun?

Moon Apart from the pornography

Frank That wasn't mine; it was imaginary

Mint One last question: what made you choose Drama, Frank?

Frank Um, my parents think it's a totally useless subject so it seemed like the obvious choice

Mint OK. Well done. Respect. Round of applause

Only Mint and Ella clap.

Briggs Frank

Frank Yes?

Briggs I love you

Frank flinches as if he's about to be hit.

[...]

B3 Read the info-box and explain the following quotation: "The text of a play is like the score of a symphony – a finished work, yet only a potentiality until it is performed". Consider what you have already learned in sections A and B to bring a play to life.

Info: Drama
Unlike novels or short stories, plays are not written to be read but to be performed on stage. A play is no more than a script that has to be brought to life as it only contains the dialogue and some stage directions. The recipient is directly confronted with the characters as there is no narrator who explains or interprets characters and situations. Consequently, plays are open to diverging interpretations.

Analysis

Skills
How to write a text analysis p. 83

B4 a) Mint decides to let Frank be himself on the hot seat. Describe and explain the students' reaction to Mint's decision.
In order to do this task consider the following aspects:

- **Dialogue:** Which students show any reaction to Mint's decision?
  → Only Moon, he calls Mint's decision "psychological torture" (l. 56).
  What else does he say and what does it reveal about his opinion of Mint's decision?
- **Stage directions:** What do the stage directions reveal about the students' reaction?
  → As Moon is the only student who protests against Mint's decision, what do the stage directions reveal about the other students' reactions?

b) Analyze how the language of both Mint and his students creates atmosphere. In order to do this task find answers to the following questions:

- **Dialogue: What does the choice of words indicate?**
  → Mint: He uses deprecating words for his students, for example "spoilt rebels and fashion victims" (ll. 9–10). This indicates that Mint is rather disrespectful of his students. Find more examples.
  → His students: Point, for example, expresses doubts about Mint's future at the school: "No, Mint, why don't we see how long you last?" (ll. 23–24). Again, mutual disrespect becomes obvious.
  What is the nature of the dialogue?
  → The dialogue takes place during a drama lesson at school. The students demonstrate their lack of motivation while the teacher resorts to irony when he says "We're off to a great start already" (l. 25). Find other examples in which language contributes towards creating atmosphere in the classroom.
- **Pace: What is the pace of this extract?**
  → As the dialogue predominantly consists of rather short questions and equally short replies, the pace is quite fast in this extract.

Language support

atmosphere

The atmosphere can be described as …
A hostile/relaxed/tense atmosphere is created by …
The pace of the extract suggests that the atmosphere is …
The prevailing atmosphere is …
The … creates an atmosphere of ….
The atmosphere evokes feelings of …/fits in with …/foreshadows …/creates suspense …

Language support

Useful adjectives:

positive:
enjoyable, peaceful, calm, lively, comfortable, cheerful, relaxed, pleasant, harmonious, idyllic, picturesque, familiar, friendly, warm

negative:
grave, tense, unpleasant, disagreeable, dark, gloomy, dismal, dreary, depressing, desolate, discouraging, hopeless, cheerless, bleak

Checklist: Analyzing drama

When analyzing the script of a play, only the **dialogue** and possibly some **stage directions** offer answers to questions that help interpret and eventually produce the play. However, it's also important to pay attention to the following:

✓ **Plot and plot structure:** What happens in the play? What is the structure of the play? What techniques does the playwright use?
✓ **Themes:** What ideas are expressed in the play? What does the playwright tell us about the world and ourselves?
✓ **Characters:** Who are the characters in the play? What do they do? How do they feel? What conflicts are there? What are their relationships? What are their personal traits?
✓ **Setting:** What is the world of the play? Where does it happen? When does it happen?
✓ **Language in dialogues or monologues:** What does the choice of words indicate? What is the context and the nature of the dialogue? How are allusions and imagery used?
✓ **Pace:** What is the pace of the scene/play?
✓ **Atmosphere:** How is atmosphere created? How does the interaction of the characters/the language/the setting contribute to the atmosphere?

Comment/Creative writing

B5 Comment on Mint's understanding of his professional role as a drama teacher. Take into consideration his relationship to his students.

Skills
How to write a comment
p. 84–85

B6 Continue the dialogue: Now Moon is in the hot seat and his classmates ask him questions. In order to do this task consider the following aspects:

- **Characters:** Study Moon's role in the extract and identify his personal traits.
- **Themes:** Decide what Moon's classmates might want to find out about him.
- **Language:** Choose appropriate language (register, choice of words) for the students as well as for Mint.
- Include **stage directions** that indicate how the characters should behave.

Skills
How to write creatively
p. 86–87

Getting to the point

Comprehension

Skills
How to write a summary p. 82

C1 Read the extract from "Citizenship" by Mark Ravenhill below. Briefly summarize the extract and describe the different interests of the two characters.

Analysis

Skills
How to write a text analysis p. 83

C2 Analyze the dialogue between Tom and de Clerk and explain the means the playwright uses to create atmosphere.

Comment/Creative writing

Skills
How to write a comment p. 84–85

C3 Comment on the advice de Clerk gives to Tom at the end of the extract (ll. 131–139).

Skills
How to write creatively p. 86–87

C4 Add a scene: Although Tom has still not spoken to someone who he knows is homosexual, he has taken de Clerk's advice and decided to come out at school and make public that he is gay. Despite some neutral and even positive reactions from some of his classmates, Tom is seriously bullied by others and, consequently, desperate for help and support. He talks to his teacher de Clerk again. Write their dialogue and include appropriate stage directions.

The following Extract is again taken from Mark Ravenhill's play "Citizenship" and set at school: Tom has made a mess of his coursework because he got some blood on it from a minor injury. He now has to rewrite it to make it look neat again. Mr de Clerk is his highly stressed teacher.

[...]

De Clerk's mobile rings.

Tom You gonna get that, sir?

De Clerk No.

Mobile stops.

Tom Might have been important.

De Clerk Nothing else matters. Nothing else matters but your coursework and the inspectors and that we don't become a failing school, okay? There is nothing else in the whole wide world that matters apart from that.

Mobile rings again.

Tom They don't think so.

De Clerk Well fuck 'em, fuck 'em, fuck 'em.

Tom They really want to talk to you.

De Clerk Uhhh. *(Answers the mobile.)* No. Still at – I told you. I told you – because we've got the inspectors. No. No. Well put it in the fridge and I'll ... put it in the bin. I don't care. I don't care. I can't.

De Clerk ends the call.

Tom Are you married, sir?

De Clerk I'm not talking any more.

Tom I was just wondering.

De Clerk Well, don't.

Tom Other teachers say: my wife this or my girlfriend that. But you never do.

De Clerk Well, that's up to them.

Tom It makes you wonder. We all wonder.

De Clerk Listen, I'm here from eight in the morning until eight in the evening, midnight the last few weeks – maybe I don't have a personal life.

Tom Yeah.

De Clerk Maybe I'm not a person at all. Maybe I'm just lesson plans and marking.

Tom Yeah. Maybe.

De Clerk Oh. My head. Have you got a Nurofen[1]?

Tom Sorry, sir?

De Clerk Have you got a Nurofen or something?

[1] **Nurofen** = brand name of a range of pain-relief medication

Tom No, sir. I had some but I took them all.

De Clerk Right.

Tom If you want to go home – go home to your ... partner.

De Clerk I can't.

Tom I can do a massage, sir. I know how to do a massage.

De Clerk No.

Tom It stops headaches. I done it loads of times.

De Clerk Listen. Physical contact is –

Tom Out of lessons now.

De Clerk Difficult.

Tom Sssssshhhh. Our secret.

Tom moves over to de Clerk and massages his shoulders and neck.

You've got to breathe too. Remember to keep breathing.

De Clerk Mmm.

Tom There's a lot of stress about, isn't there?

De Clerk It's all stress.

Tom How old are you?

De Clerk Twenty-two.

Tom Lots of teachers burn out before they're twenty-five because of all the stress.

De Clerk Mmm.

Tom You're quite developed, sir. Do you go to the gym?

De Clerk Sometimes.

Tom With your ... partner.

De Clerk Back to your work now. That was wrong. Physical contact.

Tom Sir – I'm really sorry, but I've –

Tom wipes de Clerk's shoulder.

I've dripped on you, sir.

De Clerk What?

Tom You've got blood on your shirt.

De Clerk Oh, fuck.

Tom I'm really sorry. It's a really nice shirt.

De Clerk Shit. Shit. Shit.

De Clerk scrubs at his shoulder.

Tom If you want me to get you another one, sir –

De Clerk No no.

Tom I get a discount. My brother manages Top Man[2].

De Clerk Tom – get on with your work. You get on with your work and I'll get on with my work.

Tom You've got good clothes, sir. For a teacher.

De Clerk Tom.

Pause.

Tom Sir ... I keep on having this dream and in this dream I'm being kissed.

De Clerk Don't.

Tom Only I never know whether it's a man or woman whose doing the kissing.

De Clerk This isn't Biology. I'm Citizenship.

Tom I think I dream about being kissed by a man.

De Clerk I don't want to know about that.

Tom I really want to know: do I dream about a man kissing me?

De Clerk Please. Don't do this. I'm tired. I'm exhausted. I've got the Head of Department chasing me. I've got the inspectors coming after me like wolves after blood. I've still got eight hours of paperwork and I've done a full day's teaching. Please understand the pressure I'm under and just copy the work.

Tom What do you do if you're gay, sir?

De Clerk You talk to someone.

Tom I'm trying to talk to you.

De Clerk You don't talk to me. Talk to your form tutor.

Tom He hates me.

De Clerk I don't think so.

Tom What do you do at the weekends, sir?

De Clerk Alright. Go away. Go home.

Tom What about the coursework?

De Clerk I'll explain the blood to the inspectors.

Tom Alright then.

Tom packs up his bag.

Bye then, sir.

De Clerk Bye, Tom.

Tom I want to talk to someone gay, sir. I don't know any.

De Clerk Shut up, please shut up.

Tom I really want to meet someone gay and ask them what it's like.

De Clerk Well – it's fine. It's normal. It's just fine.

Tom You reckon?

De Clerk You know the school policy: we celebrate difference. You report bullies. Everything's okay. You're okay.

Tom I don't feel okay.

De Clerk Well – you should do.

[...]

[2] **Top Man** = a clothing store for men

How to write a summary

If someone asks you to tell them about a book or an article you have read, they don't expect you to tell them everything. What they want is a short version or summary. A written summary only gives the information that a reader needs to get a general idea of what the text is about.

Read the text thoroughly, divide it up into parts and look for keywords before you start writing your summary. This will make it easier for you to use your own words in the summary and to leave out unnecessary details.

Dos	In the introduction include the author, title, type of text and year of publication. ✓ State the topic of the text, i.e. the underlying conflict/problem, etc., and not simply its content. ✓ Focus on the basic facts. ✓ Use the present tense. ✓ Present events in chronological order. ✓ Use your own words. ✓ Use connectives to link your sentences. Look at page 100 for help. ✓ Use formal language.
Don'ts	✓ Don't give too many details. ✓ Don't use the past tense. ✓ Don't use quotations or direct speech. ✓ Don't give your personal opinion. ✓ Don't start analyzing the text. ✓ Don't create suspense.
Language support	**Introduction:** ✓ *The short story/novel/article/poem … "[title]" …* ✓ *The extract from the … "[title]" …* ✓ *… by [author] …* ✓ *… written by [author] in [year]…* ✓ *… written by [author] and published in [year/source]…* ✓ *… deals with/is about/shows/deals with the question of [topic].* **Stating the topic/purpose of a text:** ✓ *The text/story … is about/shows/presents/depicts/alludes to/refers to/ criticizes/targets/comments on/exposes … the fact that/the problem of …*

How to write a text analysis

When writing a text analysis, analyzing chronologically often seems easier, but can be problematic if your task is to concentrate on a certain aspect of the text you are analyzing. Plan your text well before you start writing your analysis to find out whether a chronological or an aspect-oriented analysis works better! If you are supposed to analyze a development, for example, a chronological analysis might work better, if you are examining a certain character, you should concentrate on relevant aspects.
Always examine the (stylistic/rhetorical/structural/ ...) devices the author uses and explain why they are used/what they support and what their effect on the reader is.

Dos	✓ Begin with a central claim. In order to do that, keep the central message or problem of the text in mind, but also the task you are working on. ✓ Structure your text logically; analyze the text either chronologically or aspect-oriented. ✓ Distinguish between types of texts. When you analyze prose, for example, narrative techniques are especially important. When you analyze poetry, pay special attention to rhyme and rhythm. And when you analyze non-fictional texts, the argumentative structure may be the most relevant aspect. ✓ Give examples for important stylistic devices (direct or indirect quotations), explain them/their meaning and analyze their effect on the reader. ✓ Always combine findings on language/structure and content/message. ✓ Use the present tense. ✓ Use connectives to link your ideas. Look at page 100 for help. ✓ Use formal and neutral language. ✓ End with a conclusion that doesn't only sum up your findings, but also refers back to the task and states your results on a more abstract level.
Don'ts	✓ Don't use the past tense. ✓ Don't only paraphrase the text you are analyzing. ✓ Don't speculate – you must use evidence from the text to support your findings! ✓ Don't write about every detail.
Language support	**Writing about language/style:** ✓ *formal/informal/colloquial/vulgar/sophisticated/academic/clear/objective/vivid/exaggerated/… language* ✓ *complex/simple sentences* ✓ *a serious/friendly/humorous/ironic/polite/rude/critical/optimistic/… tone* ✓ *The style of the text is plain/condensed/vivid/pompous/artificial/…* **Writing about stylistic/rhetorical devices:** ✓ *The author uses metaphorical language to …* ✓ *The author employs stylistic devices to …* ✓ *The author uses figures of speech to …* ✓ *The stylistic devices underline/enhance the arguments/message of the text.* ✓ *The stylistic device supports/affirms the author's/the text's message.* ✓ *The stylistic device/metaphor/… brings out/creates additional significance/the message …* ✓ *to describe/depict …* ✓ *to examine/explain/analyze the stylistic devices* ✓ *to make a comparison ...* **Writing about characters, atmosphere, situations:** ✓ *to make use of/use … to create a … atmosphere*

How to write a comment

In a comment you are asked to give your opinion and explain it. This could be in response to something that has happened or on the views expressed in a newspaper article, discussion etc.

Dos	**Plan the structure of your comment to include the following parts.** **Introduction:** ✓ State which topic/question you will write about by referring to the task. ✓ Try to get your reader's attention by starting in an interesting way. **Main part:** ✓ Identify and refer to the arguments put forward in the text. ✓ Clearly state your own opinion on the topic. ✓ Weigh up and reply to arguments that do not support your point of view. ✓ Include evidence to support/refute arguments (expert opinions; statistics etc.). ✓ Base your arguments on facts and put them forward coherently and unemotionally – that is more convincing. verbunden **Conclusion:** ✓ Sum up your arguments. ✓ Come to a logical conclusion about the topic/question stating your opinion. **Organize your ideas coherently:** ✓ Organize your ideas into paragraphs. ✓ Link your ideas/paragraphs with connectives. Look at page 100 for help. **Use formal language:** ✓ Use connectives (*in addition, finally, moreover, however,* etc.). ✓ Use the passive voice occasionally. ✓ Try to avoid using "I" too frequently. There are many other ways of expressing your opinion.
Don'ts	✓ Don't start writing before you have planned your answer and know what conclusion you will come to. ✓ Don't just state arguments/opinions without supporting them. ✓ Don't use informal language, e.g. short forms (*don't, can't*, etc.), colloquial language (*kids, gonna*, etc.) or slang.

Language support

Referring to the topic/question in the introduction:

- ✓ *This comment/answer will discuss/consider/argue …*
- ✓ *The problem/issue to be discussed in this comment is …*
- ✓ *The text/article/story/author … raises the question of/introduces the problem of …, which will be discussed in this comment.*

Identifying and referring to arguments for the main part:

- ✓ *The main problem/issue/question that is touched upon in this article is …*
- ✓ *The author states/argues/claims/maintains/supports the idea/puts forward the argument/denies the fact/contradicts the opinion that …*

Presenting your own opinion:

- ✓ *It is my belief/opinion that …/In my opinion …/Personally …*
- ✓ *As far as I can see/am concerned …/As I see it …*
- ✓ *I (completely) agree/(absolutely) disagree with …*
- ✓ *As opposed to … I (strongly) believe that …*

Weighing up and countering arguments:

- ✓ *Taking into account what has been said so far, I …*
- ✓ *Having considered the different arguments, I …/Considering the fact that …*
- ✓ *On the one hand …, on the other hand …*
- ✓ *Whereas girls generally like to use the Internet to keep in touch with friends, boys prefer to use it to play computer games./In contrast to A, B …*
- ✓ *Looking at the problem from A's side, you have to admit that …*
- ✓ *Another important point/factor/argument to consider is …*
- ✓ *Supporters/Opponents of … argue/might argue that …*
- ✓ *Others claim/assert that …*
- ✓ *While there is no doubt/question that …, … must also be considered/mentioned.*
- ✓ *It must also be taken into consideration that …*

Coming to a conclusion:

- ✓ *All in all, …/In conclusion, …*
- ✓ *To conclude, …/To sum up, …*

How to write creatively

You may be asked to continue a prose text you have read or write a passage from the point of view of one of the characters in the story. You need to write in a similar way as the author. Pay attention to the author's style and the developments in the story. Decide if your development is plausible and fits in with what has happened before.

Dos	**A. Continuation of a prose text** **Content:** ✓ Stay in line with the plot and atmosphere. ✓ You are not entirely free as you are expected to show in your text production that you have digested the original text. So you have to use the information from that text as a basis for a plausible sequel. ✓ Mention certain features (places, details of landscape or weather) that have been introduced. ✓ Make sure you present the characters in a way that does not contradict their previous behaviour unless this change in character is part of your story. ✓ If possible refer back to events in the text you have dealt with. **Point of view (narrative perspective):** ✓ Adopt the same narrative perspective: • First person or third person narrator • Omniscient (knowing and commenting on all the characters' thoughts and feelings, foreshadowing future events) or limited (having an insight into one of the character's thoughts and feelings only) **Language:** ✓ Stay in line with the author's style and try to imitate it. ✓ Consider the amount of narrative, descriptive as opposed to dramatic passages that mainly consist of dialogue. ✓ Use either long, elaborate sentences or short simple ones like the author. ✓ Employ imagery (symbolic or metaphorical language) if it occurs in the original text; you need not always think of new images but pick up the ones used and extend them. ✓ Follow the author's use of language to place a character in a particular social class or reveal his/her emotions.

Dos	**B. Change of perspective** ✓ You may be asked to consider the fictional situation from the point of view of a different character. This can be done in • a dialogue. • a diary entry/an interior monologue. • a letter to a friend. **Content:** ✓ Consider the relationship between the characters involved, their age, their social standing, the way they might be personally affected by what has happened. ✓ Imagine how they would feel in the circumstances. **Language:** ✓ Age, relationship, social class and profession determine the way a person speaks. ✓ Make sure you use an appropriate register (formal, informal, colloquial, scientific, educated). ✓ Emotions may alter a person's behaviour and speech. ✓ Use typical elements of spoken language like exclamations, incomplete sentences (ellipses), questions, etc.
Don'ts	✓ Don't stray from the original text you were given. ✓ Don't create an entirely new universe. ✓ Don't write in your personal style, but adopt the style of the author. ✓ Don't quote when you refer back to instances in the original text. Make the references part of your own narrative.
Language support	✓ In a prose text you can reveal the speaker's feelings not only in his/her words but also in his/her body language, you could even contrast the two levels. ✓ The following verbs can help you: *admit, agree, whisper, shout, cry, scream, deny, accept, convince, persuade, shrug, stammer, nod, wince, declare, laugh, smile, grin, smirk, confide, concede, frown, mutter, mumble, insult, accuse, wink,* etc.

How to write an informal letter

The level of informality will depend on who you are writing to. There will be a difference in the way you write to, e.g. a teacher or a friend. Try to picture the person you are writing to. Imagine the things that you would say to him/her and write them down. Write about personal things and thoughts.

Dos	**Plan the structure of your letter to include the following parts:** **Introduction and salutation:** ✓ Write your address (without your name) in the top right-hand corner (optional). ✓ Write the date below your address (optional). ✓ Include salutation, e.g. *Hi …,; Dear …,* ✓ Write a (few) general introductory sentence(s) in which you may: • Say why you are writing. • Ask about the recipient's health/state of mind. • Refer to a letter that you have received. **Main part:** ✓ Organize your ideas in paragraphs. ✓ Make the content lively and interesting. ✓ Use anecdotes and refer to personal experiences. **Conclusion:** ✓ Write a closing sentence, e.g. *Look forward to hearing from you soon.* ✓ Finish in an informal way, e.g. *Love …* **Try to be as conversational as possible.** ✓ Use informal language: • Short forms, e.g. *I'll, couldn't* • Colloquial language, e.g. *I guess …, to be quite honest, …* • Incomplete sentences (ellipsis), e.g. *Glad you could come!* • Emphasize the personal level by using *we, you, I.* • Use informal punctuation such as dashes "–" and exclamation marks.
Don'ts	✓ Don't forget to start the first paragraph with a capital letter. ✓ Don't neglect punctuation. ✓ Don't forget to structure your letter even if it's informal. Use simple linking devices, e.g. *then, so.*
Language support	**Say why you are writing.** ✓ *Just wanted to let you know that we are all well and thinking of you.* ✓ *Hope this letter arrives in time for your birthday.* ✓ *Thank you so much for the present.* **Inquiring about health/state of mind:** ✓ *Hope you are (keeping) well.* **Referring to a letter:** ✓ *Just a few lines to say how pleased we were to hear from you.* ✓ *Sorry it's taken me such a long time to reply to your last letter.* ✓ *We were so pleased to hear about …* ✓ *It was lovely to hear from you.* **Finishing a letter:** ✓ *(I) look forward to hearing from you soon. / Can't wait to read your next letter.* ✓ *Hope to see you in the near future.* ✓ *Take care.* ✓ *Love …/All my love …/Best wishes …/Yours …*

How to write a letter to the editor

Readers of newspapers often write a letter to the editor to comment on something they have read, usually in the hope that the letter will be published in that newspaper. When writing a letter to the editor, take the aspects for writing a formal letter into account. Use formal language, but include strong statements. Before you start writing the letter, you will need to note down important facts and points from the text you are reacting to. Maybe you can think of other ideas that could come in handy and arrange them in a logical order.

Dos	**Introduction:** ✓ Start with *Sir or Madam:* ✓ Leave out any introductory or closing remarks with which you show your politeness or personal interest. Concentrate instead on the point you are trying to make. ✓ Name the article you refer to at the beginning of your letter. ✓ Give the reason why you are writing the letter, i.e. what you support/criticize/would like to comment on about the article. **Main part:** ✓ Follow a clear line of argumentation and stick to the most important point(s). ✓ Support your arguments with evidence and examples. **Conclusion:** ✓ End with a final statement that sums up your position or provides an outlook on what you expect from future articles on the issue. ✓ Just sign your name and state your place of residence at the end.
Don'ts	✓ Don't use *Dear …* at the beginning or *Yours sincerely/faithfully* at the end. ✓ Don't quote from the original article unless it is absolutely necessary. ✓ Don't retell the article and explain it to the editor, but explain your view.
Language support	**Starting the letter:** ✓ *I am writing to you in response to the article …* ✓ *Having read your article …, I would like to point out …* ✓ *In your article …, you claim that …* ✓ *Your article … raises the question of whether …* **Expressing your opinion in the main part of the text:** ✓ *I would like to congratulate you on …* ✓ *I personally believe that …* ✓ *I could not have put it better myself.* ✓ *It is beyond doubt that …* ✓ *You are absolutely right when you say …/I utterly agree with you that …* ✓ *I wholeheartedly endorse …* ✓ *As a firm believer in …/As a supporter of …, I totally agree/I see no reason why …* ✓ *Although I understand why …, I cannot accept your overall conclusion that …* ✓ *I see your point, but I still feel that …* ✓ *I think you are mistaken if you believe …* ✓ *What you need to keep in mind is …* ✓ *I would question the argument that …* ✓ *You overlook the fact that …* **Ending with a strong statement:** ✓ *The question can no longer be whether …, but …* ✓ *However, doesn't the evidence I have cited prove that …?* ✓ *All in all, there can be no doubt that …* ✓ *Ultimately, what matters is (that) …*

How to write a diary entry

In a diary entry you write about personal experiences, thoughts and feelings. Write the events in chronological order. This will make your diary entry sound more authentic. Imagine you are having an interior monologue (= talking to yourself) or writing to your best friend (who's called diary). You can exaggerate, especially concerning your feelings.

Dos	**Plan the structure of your diary entry to include the following parts:** **Introduction and salutation:** ✓ Write the date, e.g. *3rd March, 2011* (usually in the top right-hand corner). ✓ Begin with the salutation *Dear Diary*. ✓ Write a general introductory sentence. This could be a description of your general state of mind. **Main part:** Write chronologically about ✓ what happened (to you), what you experienced. ✓ how you felt and feel about it. ✓ include your dreams, hopes and secrets. **Conclusion:** ✓ Close with a concluding sentence, e.g. a reflection on your day or what you have written/how it has helped you. ✓ Write your name at the end – you can also add *Bye* or *Goodnight*, but this is optional.
Don'ts	✓ Don't be too formal and complicated. ✓ Don't get lost in detail – your diary will not include things you are not interested in and/or were not involved in. ✓ Don't simply describe but write down your thoughts and opinions about events, people etc.
Language support	**Use informal language:** ✓ Short forms, e.g. *I'll, couldn't* ✓ Colloquial language, e.g. *kind of, maybe* ✓ Incomplete sentences, e.g. *Worked hard today!* ✓ Exclamations, e.g. *Why bother? Brilliant! Awesome! Wicked!* **Use connectives to organize your ideas:** *besides, so, anyway, all the same, all the more so because, (un)fortunately, happily/funnily/strangely enough* **Ideas for an introductory sentence:** ✓ *Life will never be the same again.* ✓ *Something dreadful/incredible happened today.* ✓ *I still can't believe it really happened.* ✓ *I'm over the moon!* ✓ *Why do those things always happen to me?* **To express your personal hopes and wishes:** ✓ *If only …, I really/sincerely hope that …, Hopefully …, I feel hopeful that …* ✓ *I wish … /It's my one real wish to …* ✓ *Just my luck to …* **Ideas for a concluding sentence:** ✓ *Well, that's all for now! I need to get some sleep.* ✓ *Writing all this down helps me feel better.* ✓ *I really don't know what to do about this, I'm desperate!*

How to write a speech

When you give a speech, you are aiming to get people to agree with your views. As your speech will only be heard and not read by your audience, you have to be careful how you present what you have to say. Speeches are meant to be spoken, so your language should not be too formal. You may use short forms and contractions like *don't, we're, haven't, I'm,* etc. It may help you to read out aloud to yourself what you have written to check whether your style creates the desired effect.

Dos	**Plan the structure of your speech to include the following parts:** **Introduction:** ✓ Directly address the audience at the beginning. ✓ Begin your introduction with an "attention-getter" to capture your audience's attention, e.g. a story, a rhetorical question, a quotation. ✓ Clearly state the topic of your speech and your personal stance on it. **Main part:** ✓ Explain the topic/problem. ✓ Quote facts and people to persuade your audience. ✓ Show your emotional involvement and appeal to the emotions of the audience. **Conclusion:** ✓ Briefly highlight your main points and end with something strong, e.g. an appeal for support. ✓ Show that the speech has ended, e.g. by thanking your audience for listening.
Don'ts	✓ Don't put too many ideas in your speech, but give the listeners two or three important things to remember. ✓ Don't just read the speech out aloud to your audience. ✓ Don't use too complex expressions. ✓ Don't write very long sentences – listeners must be able to follow you. ✓ Don't use modifiers, e.g. *might be, possibly, probably, more or less,* – you must be very direct and specific to be convincing.
Language support	**Introduction:** ✓ Address the audience: *ladies and gentlemen, fellow students, my friends, members of …, my fellow countrymen, comrades,* etc. **Main part:** ✓ Relate your speech to your listeners. Use receiver-including pronouns and words like *we, us, our, my friends,* etc. ✓ Use connectives to structure your speech: *firstly, finally,* etc. Look at page 100 for help. ✓ Link the different points by using phrases such as: *Having discussed … it is now appropriate to mention …* ✓ Use adverbial phrases to underline your own convictions and win over the audience: *undoubtedly, certainly, undeniably, definitely, indeed, paradoxically, surprisingly, strangely enough, primarily, first and foremost, above all,* etc. ✓ Include rhetorical questions like: *Don't we all agree/want to …?* ✓ Include rhetorical devices like repetitions, exaggerations, alliterations, etc. **Conclusion:** ✓ *Finally, fellow friends of the environment, …* ✓ Clearly indicate the end of your speech: *Thank you for your attention, ladies and gentlemen.*

How to work with cartoons

Cartoons are often used to make a critical comment on a serious issue in a humorous way. They are often published in newspapers or magazines. In order to understand the cartoon it is important to look at every detail, and you should consider the connection between the picture, the punch line and any speech bubbles.

Issue
Before you study the cartoon in detail, decide what the issue is.

Presentation of characters
Are the characters in the cartoon caricatures of real people like politicians or other persons of public interest, or do they stand for a particular group?

Scene/Setting
What is the situation depicted in the cartoon? Where is it set? Who are the characters involved? What are they doing?

The cat had figured out how to work Ebay.

Source
The cartoon may be published in a newspaper or a magazine. What is the general attitude represented by the paper? Is it more conservative or more liberal? When was the cartoon first published?

Punch line or written comment
Is the punch line presented as direct speech or as a general statement? Does it contain a play on words or a double meaning? Does it suggest a parallel to past or present situations or events?

Language support	
Describing cartoons	Interpreting cartoons
• At the top/bottom of the cartoon ... • In the foreground/background ... • On the right/left ... • In the centre ... • In the top/bottom right-hand/left-hand corner ... • The cartoonist shows ... • There are ... in the picture. • The situation reminds one/me/you of ... • The cartoon describes ...	• The expression on the girl's face shows fear. • The boys are standing close together. This could mean that ... • She is hugging him. That suggests ... • By presenting ..., the cartoonist ...

How to quote

When you analyze a text, you need quotations from that text to support your statements and findings with evidence.
You can quote directly or indirectly, and you can integrate quotations into your own sentences or quote passages to back up what you have said in your own words.

You may ...	Examples
1) ... quote indirectly from a text, i.e. say something that can be found in the text in your own words. This is often used when stating facts that need no in-depth interpretation. To show that you haven't quoted directly from the text, use "cf."[1].	Ed works as a taxi driver and plays cards with his friends Audrey and Marvin on a regular basis (cf. p. 58).
2) ... integrate direct quotes into your own sentence. But be careful: don't change the meaning of the quotation, and make sure the resulting sentence is grammatically correct. To show that you are quoting directly from the text, use inverted commas.	Ed comes from one of the parts of the town where the poorer, less educated people live, which he himself describes as a "dirty secret" (p. 59).
3) ... quote a short passage or sentence directly to back up what you have already said in your own words. Again, use inverted commas to show that it is a direct quotation.	Ed states clearly that he is not content with his life: "No real career. No respect in the community. Nothing" (p. 58).

[1] **cf.** = from the Latin word *confer* meaning "compare"; used for referring to sth. that is connected with the subject that is being written about

When you quote from a text, ...

- don't quote very long passages. Quotes should underline or support what you have to say, not say it for you.
- don't use quotes simply to fill paper space – they must refer to your findings.
- quote the exact wording and punctuation from the text. If you leave something out or change something to make it fit into your sentence, you have to indicate that clearly by using [...]. You may only make minor changes and mustn't alter the meaning of your quote.
- don't use quotations to retell a text or story.
- make sure the quotes are meaningful – don't quote the first two words followed by "...".
- always refer to lines or pages (l. 1/ll. 5–7/p. 8/pp. 8–9 etc.). Use "l." for one line, "ll." for more than one line, "p." for one page and "pp." for more than one page.
- you should set off the quoted passage further away from the left-hand margin if the quoted text is more than two or three sentences long.

How to improve your text

Once you have written your text, read it carefully again and check whether you have considered the criteria listed below. Revise your text accordingly.

a) Content:

- Has your text taken all aspects of the assignment into consideration?
- Have you given evidence to support your arguments?
- Have you referred adequately to the text that has to be analyzed (lines, quotations)?
- Have you avoided repetitions?

b) Structure and logical order:

Are the following parts included?

- introduction, introductory sentence
- main part
- conclusion

Is the text clearly structured and therefore easy to follow with the help of

- connectives? Look at page 100 for help.
- visible paragraphs?
- a clear order of arguments or examples?

c) Language and style:

- Have you used the correct tense, e.g. present tense in a summary?
- Have you used the correct language, e.g. formal language in a letter to the editor?
- Are your sentences complete and not too long or complicated?
- Do appropriate linking words connect ideas and sentences to make your text coherent?
- Have you avoided waffling, i.e. excluded all unnecessary words?
- Have you varied your vocabulary by using synonyms?

Language support

Improving your style by expressing yourself more precisely (adjectives and nouns)
Apart from using sentence links to structure and organize a text, there is another way to improve your style: Simply ban the following from your range of vocabulary – at least when writing a formal text like an analysis or characterization:

SAD HAPPY NICE BAD INTERESTING SITUATION

There are various synonyms you might use instead – here are a few examples:

- For "sad" people you could use:
  downcast, depressed, downhearted, dejected, dispirited, frustrated, discouraged, sorrowful

- For "sad" atmosphere you could use:
  dark, gloomy, dismal, dreary, depressing, desolate, melancholy, hopeless, cheerless, bleak

- For "happy" people you could use:
  cheerful, contented, relaxed, pleased, delighted, light-hearted, jolly, merry, lively, vivacious, animated, buoyant, humorous, spirited

- For "nice" people you could use:
  amiable, kind-hearted, good-natured, gentle, congenial, easy-going, pleasant, sympathetic
- For "nice" atmosphere you could use:
  cheerful, relaxed, pleasant, harmonious, idyllic, picturesque, familiar, friendly, warm
- For "bad" people you could use:
  despicable, contemptible, loathsome, hateful, detestable, reprehensible, awful, vile, mean, repulsive, horrible, dreadful, terrible
- For "interesting" you could use:
  appealing, exciting, fascinating, remarkable, significant, captivating, intriguing, attractive
- For "situation" you could use:
  circumstance, case, state of affairs, condition, predicament, position, dilemma

Language support

Writing about the author's opinion, point of view, bias ...
When writing about or referring to the author of the text you have to analyze, you should not only write "the author says" but use more precise alternatives instead. Here are several examples of verbs you could use:

The author ...

refers to ...
alludes to ...
talks about/mentions ...
addresses the issue of -ing ...
examines ...
raises the question of whether ...

doubts ...
attacks/accuses so. of -ing ...
blames sth./so. ...
criticizes ...
reproaches so. for -ing ...
rejects (the idea of) ...
abandons the idea of -ing ...
opposes the idea of -ing ...
refutes the argument ...

claims/maintains/argues that ...
assumes/supposes/presumes that ...
asserts ...
believes ...
states ...
insists ...
emphasizes ...
sides with ...
backs up his argument with ...
is in favour of -ing ...
puts forward another argument ...

weighs the arguments ...
is in two minds about ...

leaves ... unanswered ...
avoids this issue ...
does not consider ...

How to analyze statistics

Statistics can appear in different forms. Usually, they take one of the forms below:

bar chart

Americans online by age in per cent

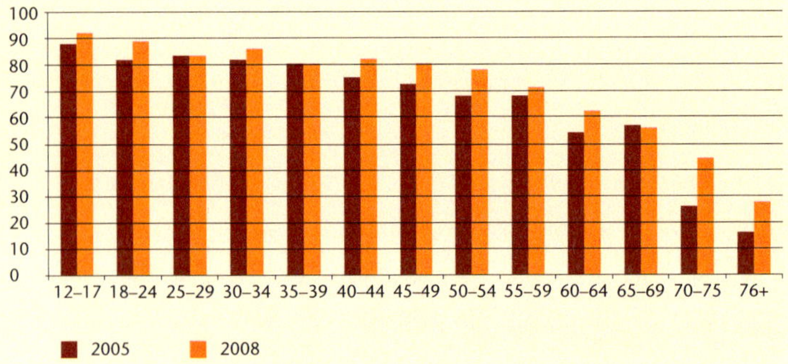

pie chart

Films teenage males have nightmares about

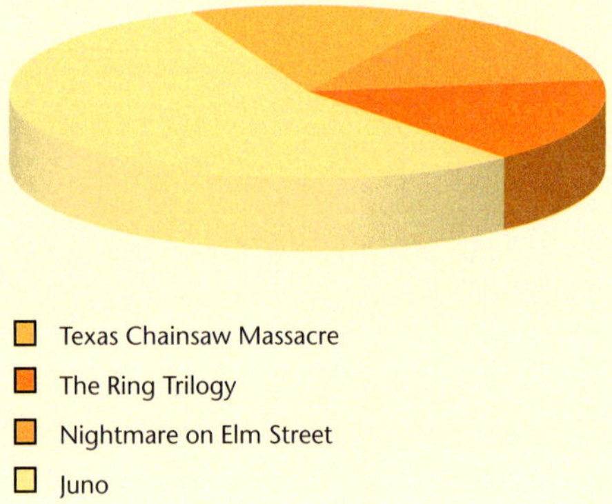

line graph

Pregnancy rate for teenagers 15–19 years old

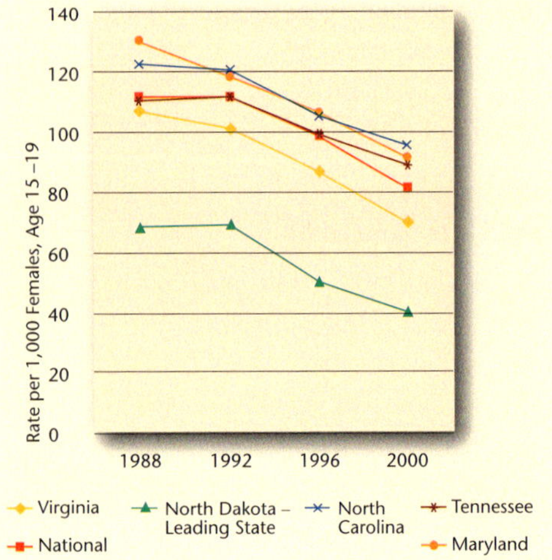

table

Teen unemployment in the US

Year	All Teens	White Teens	Black Teens	Hispanic Teens	All Workers
2001	14.7%	12.7%	29.0%	17.7%	4.7%
2002	16.5	15.5	29.8	20.1	5.8
2003	17.5	15.2	33.0	20.0	6.0
2004	17.0	15.0	31.7	20.4	5.5
2005	16.6	14.2	33.3	18.4	5.1
2006	15.4	13.2	29.1	15.9	4.6
2007	15.7	13.9	29.4	18.1	4.6
2008	18.7	16.8	31.2	22.4	5.8
2009	24.3	21.8	29.5	30.2	9.3
2010	25.9	23.2	43.0	32.2	9.6
2011	26.3	23.5	46.9	32.9	9.0

Studying the figures

1. Before you start analyzing statistics, make sure you study the graph/chart/table carefully. Find out what the statistics are about.

2. Study the legend and the figures and check if they are absolute numbers or percentages. Pay special attention to the way the figures are presented visually to make sure that proportions are represented accurately, for example.

3. Look for general trends or noteworthy figures or correlations. What you can find out depends largely on the type of visualisation. Pie charts and bar graphs usually deal with the relative size/importance of data, line graphs and tables often emphasize certain developments including peaks and troughs in trends.

Describing and interpreting the figures

Introduction: • How are the figures presented? • What is the graph/chart/table about? • What is the source of the figures?	*The graph/chart/table shows/presents/provides information on/deals with ..., covering a period of ...* *The topic/subject/theme of the graph/chart/table is ...* *It is taken from/The source of the data is ...* *The graph/chart/table was published by ...*
Description: • How do the figures develop? • What is the highest/lowest point? • What are the most striking points? • Are there any irregular figures? • If there are figures to compare, are there any similarities/differences?	*The horizontal/vertical axis shows ...* *There is a considerable/steady/sharp/slight/marked increase/decrease in the number of ...* *The number/amount/proportion of ... has changed slightly/clearly ...* *The numbers drop/fall/decrease ...* *The figures remain constant/steady ...* *The figures reach a peak/a trough in ...* *In ..., X bottomed out at 8%/peaked out at 32%.* *The average figure for ... is ...* *The pie is subdivided into segments that represent ...* *The chart/graph/table reveals/shows that ...* *The numbers for ... are about twice as high as those ...* *The ... with the highest frequency/number of ... is ...*
Conclusion and evaluation: • What general conclusion can be drawn from the figures? • What could be reasons for the figures? • How can the figures be related to each other? • What can be predicted on the basis of those figures? • How do the figures relate to what you know about the topic? Are they objective or biased?	*All in all/By and large, the statistics for ... reveal/show/... that ...* *It seems likely/unlikely that the figures for ... will (not) continue to ...* *Against the background of ..., the figures/results are (not) very surprising/revealing/enlightening ...* *The data confirm/contradict/are (not) consistent with ...* *The graph/chart/table conveys a false/one-sided impression because ...*

How to structure a text

When analyzing a text or commenting on an issue, you should not only pay attention to the content and the correct use of language (grammar, choice of words, etc.), but also to the structure of your text.
In order to write a well-structured text you should follow the structure of introduction – main part – conclusion. Make sure that you plan how to present your ideas effectively in a sequence of paragraphs before you start writing.
Moreover, you should make the relationships between your points clear by using connectives, e.g. to express cause and effect or to point out contrasts and contradictions.

The outline of a text and paragraph writing

Introduction	
Analysis • Refer back to the task, if necessary. • Make a general statement that sums up what you expect to find out.	**Example:** You are asked to write a characterization of the protagonist and give a general assessment of what he is like. *In this extract, which focuses on John's feelings about his parents, John seems to be a highly ambivalent character who pretends to be friendly to his parents on the surface, but in fact hides how much he dislikes his parents.*
Comment • Refer back to the task. a) If it is a general issue, (example 1), you need to establish a connection to that topic in your opening paragraph. b) If you are expected to comment on something that is included in the text you are working on (example 2), you need to refer back to this text. • Regardless of the context, include a thesis statement which expresses your general view on the issue.	**Example 1:** You are asked to discuss whether a gap year is worth doing after school. *Thousands of students decide to take a year off from education once they have graduated from school and do not want to start studying straight away. Although this may provide a wide variety of unforgettable experiences, I do not believe that travelling the world for a year is of much benefit for your personal development or your university studies.* **Example 2:** You are asked to comment on a character's behaviour towards his parents. *As X feels annoyed and humiliated by his parents for not allowing him to live the life of a normal teenager in this situation, it seems highly doubtful that his inability to talk to his parents openly about what bothers him will solve X's problems of unhappiness and isolation.*

Main part	
• Develop your interpretation/argumentation in the main part of your analysis/argumentation in a well-structured and logical way so that it is easy for the reader to follow what you say. • Plan beforehand how you can divide up your text into paragraphs. • Follow the PEA principle for your paragraph writing. P – point: an introductory sentence that introduces the point that you are trying to make in this paragraph so that the reader immediately knows what you are referring to. E – evidence: examples from the text (including quotations) or arguments and examples that can be used to prove your point (P). A – analysis: the explanation of examples and quotations in order to make it clear how the evidence (E) helps to prove your initial point (P).	
Analysis	**Example:** Characterization of Balram in Adiga's novel "White Tiger": *Judging from his outward appearance, one can initially identify Balram as a typical example of a low-caste servant or a poor Indian in general who slowly becomes aware of the consequences his way of dressing have on his position in society. (introducing a sequence of paragraphs)* *Wearing sandals instead of proper shoes seems to be a distinctive feature separating the rich from the poor in this context as Balram as well as the other drivers all wear sandals. Hence they can identify with the poor man wearing sandals who is refused entry to the shopping mall (cf. ll. 45ff.). As their masters could enter the mall without any problem, Balram and the other drivers realize how the inequality of Indian society manifests itself even in items of clothing.*
Comment	**Example:** Discussing how sensible it is to take a year off for a gap year: *If you choose the place where you are going wisely, you may have the chance to gain some experience in the field you would like to study or work in later. There are definitely some future medical students who assist doctors and nurses in some developing country or those who want to study science and help out in a bird sanctuary or get involved in an environmental project, for example. However, the question is whether everyone already has a clear idea of what they would like to do after their gap year and would maybe prefer to use the year to make up their minds. Even if they would like to gain some experience in the field that interests them, they might not be able to find a suitable place.*

Conclusion	
Analysis • Refer back to your opening paragraph. • Summarize your most important findings concisely.	**Example:** Characterization of Balram in Adiga's novel "White Tiger": *As a closer look at Balram's character has shown, Balram becomes aware of what makes him recognizable as a lower-caste driver and tries to leave outward appearance as well as other signs like his insufficient command of the English language behind. His new way of dressing, which imitates the style of his master, as well as his recognition that he has to give up old habits that single him out as uneducated and ill-mannered show his determination to rise above his current status.*
Comment • Refer back to your opening paragraph. • Draw a conclusion from weighing up the pros and cons in your argumentation.	**Example:** Discussing how sensible it is to take a year off for a gap year: *All in all, I'm utterly convinced that gap years do not really allow you to acquire new skills and prepare for university. Although it may serve as a character-building experience to become more independent and able to adapt to new people and circumstances, I doubt that many situations you experience while travelling around the world are realistic and that these experiences can be applied to everyday life back home. Consequently, I would never do such a gap year, but rather go abroad as part of my degree course.*

Expressing connections between points in the text

Language support

Adding and ordering points:
To begin with/First of all/ Firstly, …
Secondly, …/Then …
Last but not least …
Finally/In the end , …
All in all/To conclude/To sum up …
The most important point is/ Above all …
This also becomes evident when …/… during/… in a scene
Both … and …
… not only …, but also …
This assumption can be supported by …
This is also shown by …
Another point/Another example of … is …
In addition to that/ Additionally/ Furthermore/Moreover/ Besides/On top of that, …

Expressing a contrast:
In spite of the fact …/ Despite the fact …
Whereas …
In contrast to … , …
However, …
But nevertheless, …
On the one hand …, on the other hand …
Although …
Even though/Even if …
While it is true that …, …

Expressing cause and effect:
Due to …/Because of …/As a result of …
Therefore, …/For this reason, …
… because …
As/Since …
So/Thus …
As a consequence of this, …/ Consequently, …/This results in …
Accordingly, …

Summing up:
All in all, …/To sum up, …
As a result, …
In brief, …
In conclusion, …/ To conclude, …

How to work with a dictionary

All competences, but especially reading and writing, often involve the use of a dictionary. There are **monolingual dictionaries,** which provide definitions in English and **bilingual dictionaries,** which give you the German equivalents. Most of the time you will be using a bilingual dictionary.

English – German

When working with texts you may not always understand all the words, so you will need to refer to a dictionary. The use of the dictionary, however, may be determined by the situation you are in.

- Don't look up every single word you don't know but apply the **strategie**s you have learnt **to understand words from the context** first.
- **Limit the number of words to look up** as using the dictionary is quite time-consuming.
- Depending on the task you are given it may be necessary to **check all the words you don't understand**. If you read a novel or a longer text of course, you will need to use your strategies of understanding words from the context, from cognates etc. But sometimes you need to get a detailed understanding of the text.
- Having gone to the trouble of finding the word, try and use it to build and **extend your active vocabulary**.
  - Decide if the word may be useful for later use.
  - Collect the words you have selected in word fields.
  - Add collocations or idioms to avoid possible mistakes in future.
  - Use the newly acquired words and phrases in your homework/written texts. This is the best way to remember them.

How to look the word up properly

- Make sure you look the word up in its **correct spelling** or you may end up with an incorrect translation. Examples of this are: *board-bored, fair-fare, sail-sale.*
- Determine whether the word you are looking up is a noun, a verb, an adjective etc. and read the corresponding part of the entry. With verbs, make sure you look for the basic form.
- There may still be different meanings. Read the complete entry and decide which translation fits the context of your text best.
- Avoid mistakes by checking what grammatical construction is needed with the word you want to use, for example *used to* ***do*** as opposed to *get used to* ***doing***.

The phonetic transcription shows you how to pronounce a word correctly. It not only reflects the sound but also gives you the intonation of a word, which may be different depending on the function of the word (e.g. pre'sent *v* – 'present *n*).

n, vi, vt, adj tell you what type of word it is (noun, verb etc.). If there are abbreviations you don't understand, check the explanations in the dictionary.

The headword helps you to find the word more easily.

chest [tʃest] *n* **1.** *(torso)* Brust *f*, Brustkorb *m*; **to fold one's arm across one's** ~ die Arme vor der Brust verschränken – **2.** *(trunk)* Truhe; *(box)* Kiste – **3.** *(treasury)* Schatzkästchen

The different meanings of a word are listed under numbers. Make sure that you read the whole entry to find the meaning that fits the context.

Expressions in bold letters give you examples of how to use the word correctly in typical phrases or idioms (e.g. "heavy: ~ accent, with a ~ heart").

German – English

When writing texts you will with time want to make your phrasing more precise, varied and differentiated.

Typical needs

- **Spelling:** you are not sure how the English word you want to use is written.
  - Check for changes in spelling in different grammatical contexts.
- **Vocabulary:** you want to use a particular word.
  - Make sure you have the correct German spelling. For example: the word *Widerspruch* will be hard to find if you think it is spelt with *ie*.
  - Read through **all** the possible meanings and consider the specific lexical area in which you want to use the word. For example: the German word *Bank* can mean either *bank* or *bench* in English.
  - If collocations are given, try to use the whole phrase or a parallel construction in your own text.
- **Style: variation (synonyms/antonyms):** when writing a text and editing it you will find that you have repeated certain words.
  - Use the definitions of the German word you have looked up to find other ways in English of expressing it.

Internet dictionaries

/dict.leo.org/
/www.dict.cc/

It may seem the quickest route to use an Internet dictionary, but this often is the quickest way to making lots of mistakes: Internet dictionaries often offer a one-to-one translation which may not always fit. So don't go for the first option but check carefully in which context the respective word can be used.

Tip: Since you will have to work with a non-digital dictionary in your exams, you should practise working with one in class and at home.
- You will start to get quicker at finding words.
- You will start to get more confident in choosing the right meaning.
- You will get used to benefitting from the additional information the dictionary offers you.

Glossary – Literary terms

literary terms	definition	example
short story	a work of fiction which usually deals with one or two major characters and one major conflict. The elements of a short story are character, plot, setting and theme.	
action	everything that happens in a fictional text; events that form part of a play or film	In this scene, the action takes place in …
alliteration	→ *see political speech, p. 116*	
allusion	→ *see poetry, p. 105*	
anaphora	→ *see poetry, p. 105*	
antagonist	the main character in opposition to the protagonist of a novel	
antithesis/ contrast	→ *see political speech, p. 116*	
antonym	a word that means the opposite of another word	night – day, wet – dry, hot – cold
atmosphere	the feeling or mood created by the author through the description of events, setting, situation, etc.	"For a moment, a cloud drifted past the moon and the sky turned greenish gray."
character	a person who takes part in the action of a fictional text	Grace in Dallas Woodburn's "Red"
characterization	→ *see novel, p. 114*	
climax/crisis	the most exciting or important moment in a story, event, or situation, usually near the end. This moment determines whether the situation will improve or grow worse. *Crisis* refers to the highest point of reader interest.	
conflict	the disagreement between opposing forces which is the basis of the plot of a story or a play	
dénouement	the last part of a short story, book, play, etc. in which everything is settled	
dialogue	the words that characters speak in a fictional text, play or film	
dynamic character	→ *see novel, p. 114*	
explicit characterization	→ *see novel, p. 114*	
exposition	the first part in a fictional text that provides background information and introduces the setting, the conflict and often the main character or character(s)	
external action	the writer describes what the characters do	"Grace watched the pool of Vixen Red soak through the layers of paper towels." "Tears spilled from her eyes and *drip … drip … dripped* down her cheeks, …"

literary terms	definition	example
falling action	the part of a story or play following the crisis/ climax and leading to the dénouement or catastrophe	
flat character	→ *see novel, p. 114*	
foreshadowing	the technique of hinting at future events in such a way that the reader/viewer is prepared for them or can even anticipate them	
implicit characterization	→ *see novel, p. 115*	
internal action	the writer shows the thoughts and feelings of the characters	"… but Grace felt a smile cracking her face."
metaphor	two ideas that are normally not linked are compared in a metaphor without using "as" or "like". This creates an image in the reader's mind and makes the description more powerful.	"Her mother stood a few feet away, face turned skyward, eyes squinting against the driving BBs of water …"
mood	the feeling that the writer tries to evoke, such as excitement, anger, sadness, happiness, pity, etc.	
narrative	any writing that tells a story	
narrator	a fictitious person who tells the story in a novel or film	
omniscient narrator	a narrator knowing everything about the characters	
open ending	a structural element in fictional texts in which the conflict remains for the most part unresolved	
perspective	the point of view from which a story is presented. The story can be told by a first-person or by a third-person narrator. The narrator can be a character in or outside the story. The third-person narrator can be omniscient (knowing everything about the characters) or limited (perceiving and knowing the same things as one character, seeing through the eyes of one character).	first-person perspective third-person perspective: omniscient or limited
plot	a series of related events that make up the main story in a book, film etc.	
point of view	the relation in which the narrator stands to the story	
protagonist	the main character in a fictional text	Grace in Dallas Woodburn's "Red"
repetition	words or phrases that are used more than once in a text, catching the reader's attention	"She knew this though: she loved kites and she loved rainbows. And, above all, she loved her mother."
rising action	the part of a fictional text following the exposition and leading to the climax/turning point	
round character	→ *see novel, p. 115*	

literary terms	definition	example
setting	the place and time at which the action of a fictional text takes place	
simile	a comparison of two ideas, often linked by "as" or "like"	"Like a magic kingdom that belonged only to Grace and her mother."
static character	→ *see novel, p. 115*	
subtext	the hidden meaning in a conversation, not expressed by words, but by intonation, tone of voice, facial expression, gesture, posture	
suspense	a feeling of excitement or worry that makes a reader curious about the outcome of a fictional text	
symbol	an image that does not only stand for itself but also signifies a more abstract concept or idea	"Baby steps have a way of adding up to a lot of big steps."
tension	the feeling evoked by the conflicts of a fictional text	
theme	the main idea the writer wants to present. As the theme is usually not stated directly, the reader has to figure it out.	
turning point	the point at which the action takes a different, often unexpected direction	

poetry	a literary piece of writing characterized by musical (such as rhythm and rhyme) and literary elements (such as metaphor or simile). Poems are divided into lines and often grouped into stanzas.	
alliteration	→ *see political speech, p. 116*	
allusion	a reference to a familiar or famous historical or literary figure or event	"a King who took us to the mountaintop and pointed the way to the Promised Land" (Barack Obama refers to Martin Luther King, who explained his vision of America's future in his "I have a dream" speech.)
anaphora	the repetition of identical words or phrases at the beginning of a sentence or a line	"Nobody hurt you. Nobody turned off the light … Nobody locked the door."
antithesis	contrasting two opposites	"What you recall are impressions; we have the facts."
antonym	a word that means the opposite of another word	night – day, wet – dry, hot – cold
atmosphere	→ *see short story, p. 103*	

literary terms	definition	example
blank verse	a type of poetry without a rhyme, but with a regular metre. Usually a line has five unstressed syllables.	"To be, or not to be: that is the question: Whether 'tis nobler in the mind to suffer The slings and arrows of outrageous fortune,"
ellipsis	leaving out words to avoid repetition	"Anyone's guess."
end-stopped line	the end of a line	
enjambement	one line of poetry continuing to the next	"Nobody turned off … all night." ("We remember your childhood well", ll. 1–2)
foot	a unit of poetic meter consisting of stressed and unstressed syllables. Different combinations of stressed and unstressed syllables are possible. For example, an iambic foot has an unstressed followed by a stressed syllable.	iamb: ˘ / → ab<u>ove</u> trochee: / ˘ → <u>stan</u>dard
free verse	a poem without a fixed metre or rhyme	
iamb	a unit of poetic meter consisting of an unstressed followed by a stressed syllable	iamb: ˘ / → ab<u>ove</u>, to<u>day</u>
inversion	→ *see political speech, p. 117*	
irony	a literary style employing contrasts for humorous or rhetorical effect	"In fact, it was his last big joke before his sense of humour calcified and had to be removed."
line	a unit of verse ending in a visual or typographic break and generally characterized by its length and metre: a line of iambic pentameter	
litotes	→ *see political speech, p. 117*	
metaphor	two ideas that are normally not linked are compared in a metaphor without using "as" or "like". This creates an image in the reader's mind and makes the description more powerful.	"They blazed a trail toward freedom through the darkest of nights." (Barack Obama)
metre	the pattern of stressed and unstressed syllables. Free verse has no regular metre.	free verse: no fixed metre
mood	the feeling that the writer tries to evoke, such as excitement, anger, sadness, happiness, pity, etc.	
onomatopoeia	words that sound like their meanings	"Boom. Boom. Boom."
paradox	a statement consisting of two parts that seem to mean the opposite of each other	"I can resist anything but temptation." (Oscar Wilde)
parallelism	the repetition of sentence pattern often used to contrast	"… look at you. Look at us …"
partial rhyme	the use of words which do not quite rhyme for poetic effect	"Daddy don't leave. Turn around please."
personification	the presentation of ideas, objects or animals as persons to make them more interesting for the reader	"That carrot cake with the cream cheese icing is calling my name."
perspective	→ *see short story, p. 104*	

literary terms	definition	example
point of view	the relation in which the narrator stands to the story	
repetition	→ *see short story, p. 104*	
rhetorical question	a question which expects no answer	"What does it matter now?"
rhyme	the repetition of sounds usually at the end of two or more lines	"You've lost your head if that's how easily you're led."
rhyme scheme	the pattern created by the repetition of sound at the end of lines	abab, abba, cdcd, etc.
rhythm	the pace or "movement" of a poem. The rhythm is determined by the metre and by the length of sentences.	
simile	→ *short story, p. 105*	
stanza	a section of a poem consisting of a group of lines	
structure	the organisation of the elements of a text	
subtext	the hidden meaning in a conversation, not expressed by words, but by intonation, tone of voice, facial expression, gesture, posture	
symbol	→ *see short story, p. 105*	
theme	the main idea the writer wants to present. As the theme is usually not stated directly, the reader has to figure it out.	
tone	the tone the author uses to convey his/her attitude towards the subject	ironic, sarcastic, serious, sentimental, humorous
verse	a section of a poem consisting of a group of lines	

non-fiction	texts that give facts about real events, things or people	
bias	→ *see cartoons/non-fictional texts, p. 108*	
caption	→ *see cartoons/non-fictional texts, p. 108*	
conclusion/ concluding paragraph	the final part of an article or a piece of writing	
ellipsis	leaving out words to avoid repetition	"Anyone's guess."
enumeration	naming each one of a series or list of things	
euphemism	a word or expression that people use when they want to talk about something unpleasant or embarrassing without mentioning the thing itself. It is used to spare the reader's feelings.	
exaggeration	→ *see political speech, p. 116*	
headline	→ *see cartoons/non-fictional texts, p. 109*	
introduction	the part at the beginning of any text	
irony	a literary style employing contrasts for humorous or rhetorical effect	"In fact, it was his last big joke before his sense of humour calcified and had to be removed."

literary terms	definition	example
litotes	→ *see political speech, p. 117*	
main part/body	the body/main part of a book or document, not including the introduction or the notes	
metaphor	→ *see political speech, p. 117*	
paradox	a statement consisting of two parts that seem to mean the opposite of each other	"I can't resist anything but temptation." (Oscar Wilde)
paragraph	a section of a piece of writing that begins on a new line and contains a group of several interrelated sentences	
parallelism	→ *see poetry, p. 106*	
personification	the presentation of ideas, objects or animals as persons to make them more interesting for the reader	"That carrot cake with the cream cheese icing is calling my name."
point of view	the relation in which the narrator stands to the story, a mental viewpoint or attitude	
register	the level of language (degree of formality)	formal, informal, slang, …
repetition	→ *see short story, p. 104*	
rhetorical question	→ *see political speech, p. 117*	
structure	the organisation of the elements of a text	
style	the special, often personal and individual way in which a writer expresses ideas depending on personal factors and the type of text he/she is writing	
sub-heading	the title of one section of a longer piece of writing	
subtext	the hidden meaning in a conversation, not expressed by words, but by intonation, tone of voice, facial expression, gesture, posture	
tone	→ *see poetry, p. 107*	

cartoons/non-fictional texts		
bias	a prejudice in favour of or against one thing, person or group. It is a tendency to hold a certain point of view at the expense of other alternatives. An article is biased if information is presented in a one-sided way based on personal opinion rather than facts.	
caption	words printed near or on a picture that explain sth. about the picture; a joke that is printed underneath a humorous drawing or photograph	
caricature	a presentation in which so.'s/sth.'s features are exaggerated to produce a comic or grotesque effect	
concluding paragraph	→ *see non-fiction, p. 107*	

literary terms	definition	example
euphemism	→ *see political speech, p. 116*	
exaggeration	→ *see political speech, p. 116*	
focal point	the central point in a cartoon which is of interest	
headline	the title of a cartoon, a newspaper story, etc.	
introduction	the part at the beginning of any text (exposition)	
irony	a literary style employing contrasts for humorous or rhetorical effect	"In fact, it was his last big joke before his sense of humour calcified and had to be removed."
litotes	→ *see political speech, p. 117*	
main part	the body/main part of a book or document, not including the introduction or the notes	
non-fiction	texts that give facts about real events, things or people	
paradox	a statement consisting of two parts that seem to mean the opposite of each other	"I can resist anything but temptation." (Oscar Wilde)
paragraph	a section of a piece of writing that begins on a new line and contains a group of several interrelated sentences	
personification	the presentation of ideas, objects or animals as persons to make them more interesting for the reader	"That carrot cake with the cream cheese icing is calling my name."
point of view	→ *see short story, p. 104*	
register	the level of language (degree of formality)	formal, informal, slang, …
rhetorical question	→ *see poetry, p. 107*	
subtext	the hidden meaning in a conversation, not expressed by words, but by intonation, tone of voice, facial expression, gesture, posture	
symbol	→ *see short story, p. 105*	
tone	→ *see poetry, p. 107*	

film	a series of moving pictures with sound that you can watch at the cinema or on television	
acoustic effects	effects relating to sound, e.g. in a play or a film	
action	everything that happens in a fictional text; events that form part of a play or film	In this scene, the action takes place in …
actor/actress	the person who performs in a play or film	Jesse Eisenberg as Mark Zuckerberg in "The social network"
anti-hero	a main character in a novel or drama who does not have the qualities that a hero usually has, such as idealism or being morally good	
atmosphere	→ *see short story, p. 103*	
backlighting	filming a subject or object illuminated from behind	

literary terms	definition	example
cameraman	so. who operates a camera for making films or TV programmes	
cast	noun: all the performers in a play or film verb: to choose an actor for a role in a play or film	
characterization	→ *see novel , p. 114*	
climax/crisis	the most exciting or important moment in a story, event, or situation, usually near the end. This moment determines whether the situation will improve or grow worse. *Crisis* refers to the highest point of reader interest.	
close-up	a full-screen shot of a person's face to show emotions revealed by their facial expression; it can also be used to draw attention to an object that is of particular interest to the plot or has a symbolic function.	
composer	so. who writes the music, e.g. for a film	
crane shot	the camera is placed on a crane and moves in all directions. A crane is generally used for high angle shots.	
credits	a list of people involved in the making of a film	
cross-cutting (parallel action)	combining shots of two or more scenes which are usually taking place at the same time	
cut	a quick move from one shot to the next in a film	
dialogue	the words that characters speak in a fictional text, play or film	
director (filmmaker)	so. who is in charge of making a film, or getting a play ready for performance, instructs the actors and the crew	David Fincher ("The social network")
director of photography	so. who is responsible for setting up the camera and lighting a shot	
editing (montage)	the arrangement of shots in a structured sequence	
establishing shot	gives an overall impression of the location at the beginning of a scene	
exposition	the first part in a fictional text that provides background information and introduces the setting, the conflict and often the main character or character(s)	
extreme close-up (detail shot)	shows an object in detail, emphasizing its importance in the scene	
fade-in	if a sound or picture fades in, it gradually becomes louder or clearer	
fade-out	if a sound or picture fades out, it gradually disappears	
field size (camera range)	the distance between the camera and the object filmed	

literary terms	definition	example
flashback	a scene that shows what happened in the past and thus interrupts the chronological order of the plot	
flashforward	a scene that shows what may happen in the future and thus interrupts the chronological order of the plot	
format	a term used to describe the genre of a film or television programme	
full shot	gives a view of the entire figure of a person to show action or to give an impression of a constellation of characters	
hand-held camera (handy cam)	the cameraman holds the camera in his hand when filming. This conveys a feeling of authenticity to the viewer.	
hero/heroine	the main character, protagonist, who usually has good qualities	
high angle	the camera looks down on the object so that it seems smaller, less important or inferior	
jump cut	a cut between two pictures leaving out some action	
lighting	refers to the illumination of a camera subject being filmed. The lighting may be natural or artificial, very bright (high-key lighting) or dark (low-key lighting).	
long shot	provides a view of the situation or setting from a distance	
low angle shot	the camera looks up at a person so that people seem more important, powerful or even intimidating as it shows them in a superior position	
match cut	two scenes that are connected by visual or acoustic means, e.g. a door is closed in one scene and opened in the following scene in a different context, someone is crying at the end of the first and the beginning of the second scene	
medium long shot	shows a person or people in interaction with their surroundings	
medium shot	shows a person down to the waist, often used to present two people in conversation	

literary terms	definition	example
mood	the feeling that the writer tries to evoke, such as excitement, anger, sadness, happiness, pity, etc	
overhead shot (bird's eye view)	makes an object seem less important, or gives orientation	
over-the-shoulder shot	often used to present two people in conversation: you are looking straight at one person from behind the second person	
pace	the speed at which sth. happens or is done	
pan (panning shot)	the camera moves horizontally, i.e. to the left or to the right as opposed to tilting	
perspective	→ *see short story, p. 105*	
plot	a series of related events that make up the main story in a book, film etc.	
point of view	→ *see short story, p. 105*	
point-of-view shot	assumes the perspective of one of the characters so that we seem to look through his eyes	
producer	the person who is responsible for the financing and marketing of a film	
production designer	the person who designs the set for scenes that are shot in the studio	
reverse-angle shot	a sequence of point-of-view shots in which the perspective changes from one speaker to the other	
scene	a part of an act in a play or film in which events happen in the same place or period of time	
script (screenplay)	a written description of the dialogue and action of a play or film, including basic camera directions	
scriptwriter	the person who writes the text for a film	
sequence	a series of scenes which belong together	
setting	the place and time at which the action of a fictional text takes place	
shot	a length of film without break; the smallest structural unit of a film	
sound designer	the person who creates special sounds for a film	
sound recordist	the person who records the dialogue spoken by the actors	
sound technician	the person in charge of a film's soundtrack	
soundtrack	all the recorded sound of a film (dialogue, sound and sound effects)	
special effect	an unusual image or sound that has been produced artificially	

literary terms	definition	example
static shot	the camera does not move	
still	a photograph taken from one of the scenes in a film	
storyboard	a series of pictures that the director of a film uses to plan the action that will be filmed	
straight-on angle (eye-level shot)	the camera looks straight at the person: this may suggest a neutral view, however, it can also mean that two people who are not on the same level for some reason (e.g. wealth, age, academic standing, social class) are presented as equal to each other.	
sub-plot	a plot that is subordinate to the main plot of a literary work	
subtext	the hidden meaning in a conversation, not expressed by words, but by intonation, tone of voice, facial expression, gesture, posture	
suspense	a feeling of excitement or worry that makes a reader curious about the outcome of a fictional text	
synchronisation	the technique of matching the sound with the image	
tension	the feeling evoked by the conflicts of a fictional text	
tilt (tilting shot)	the camera moves vertically, i.e. upwards or downwards as opposed to panning	
tracking shot	the camera follows a person or an object	
trailer	a short filmed advertisement for a film	
transcript	the storyboard and the complete dialogue of a film	
turning point	the point at which the action takes a different, often unexpected direction	
voice-on	the speaker is shown in the picture	
voice-off	the speaker is not shown in the picture	
voice-over	the voice of a narrator commenting on what is being shown	
zoom in/zoom out	a stationary camera seems to move closer to or further away from the object, thus focussing on it or showing it in its surroundings	

literary terms	definition	example
novel	a fairly long fictional prose narrative. Normally it has a plot which develops through the actions, speech, and thoughts of its characters.	
action	everything that happens in a fictional text; events that form part of a play or film	In this scene, the action takes place in …
allusion	→ *see political speech, p. 116*	
antagonist	the main character in opposition to the protagonist of a novel	
anti-hero	a main character in a novel or drama who does not have the qualities that a hero usually has, such as idealism or being morally good	
atmosphere	→ *see short story, p. 103*	
character	a person who takes part in the action of a fictional text	Ed Kennedy in Markus Zusak's "I am the messenger"
characterization	the way in which a writer creates characters in a book, play, film etc. The author may present his characters in two ways: directly by describing them (explicit), or indirectly through their actions, thoughts or feelings and words (implicit).	"She has yellow hair, wiry legs, the most beautiful crooked smile in the world." "I was too lazy at school." "Audrey always sits opposite me, no matter where we play." → She seems to be interested.
climax/crisis	the most exciting or important moment in a story, event, or situation, usually near the end. This moment determines whether the situation will improve or grow worse. *Crisis* refers to the highest point of reader interest.	
dénouement	the last part of a short story, book, play, etc. in which everything is settled	
dynamic character	a complex character who may change (= round character)	Ed Kennedy in Markus Zusak's "I am the messenger"
explicit characterization	direct characterization by the narrator (telling). The author tells the reader explicitly about the character's looks, traits, attitudes.	"She has yellow hair, wiry legs, the most beautiful crooked smile in the world." "I was too lazy at school."
exposition	the first part in a fictional text that provides background information and introduces the setting, the conflict and often the main character or character(s)	
external action	→ *see short story, p. 103*	
falling action	the part of a story or play following the crisis/climax and leading to the dénouement or catastrophe	
flat character	a character who does not develop in the course of the action and is often a stereotype (= static character)	Ritchie in Markus Zusak's "I am the messenger"
foreshadowing	the technique of hinting at future events in such a way that the reader/viewer is prepared for them or can even anticipate them	

literary terms	definition	example
hero/heroine	the main character, protagonist, who usually has good qualities	Ed Kennedy in Markus Zusak's "I am the messenger"
implicit characterization	indirect characterization through action, behaviour, words, feelings and thoughts (showing). You learn a lot about a character by studying what he says and does, how he behaves in certain situations and interacts with others.	"Audrey always sits opposite me, no matter where we play." → She seems to be interested.
internal action	→ *see short story, p. 104*	
irony	a literary style employing contrasts for humorous or rhetorical effect	"In fact, it was his last big joke before his sense of humour calcified and had to be removed."
mood	the feeling that the writer tries to evoke, such as excitement, anger, sadness, happiness, pity, etc	
narrative	→ *see short story, p. 104*	
narrator	→ *see short story, p. 104*	
omniscient narrator	→ *see short story, p. 104*	
open ending	a structural element in fictional texts in which the conflict remains for the most part unresolved	
paragraph	a section of a piece of writing that begins on a new line and contains a group of several interrelated sentences	
perspective	→ *see short story, p. 104*	
plot	a series of related events that make up the main story in a book, film etc.	
point of view	→ *see short story, p. 104*	
protagonist	the main character in a fictional text	
register	the level of language (degree of formality)	formal, informal, slang, …
repetition	→ *see short story, p. 104*	
rising action	the part of a fictional text following the exposition and leading to the climax/turning point	
round character	a complex character who may change (= dynamic character)	Ed Kennedy in Markus Zusak's "I am the messenger"
setting	the place and time at which the action of a fictional text takes place	
static character	a character who does not develop in the course of the action and is often a stereotype (= flat character)	Ritchie in Markus Zusak's "I am the messenger"
stream of consciousness	the thoughts of a character in a book that are expressed as they happen	
structure	the organisation of the elements of a text	
sub-plot	a plot that is subordinate to the main plot of a literary work	
subtext	the hidden meaning in a conversation, not expressed by words, but by intonation, tone of voice, facial expression, gesture, posture	

literary terms	definition	example
suspense	a feeling of excitement or worry that makes a reader curious about the outcome of a fictional text	
symbol	an image that does not only stand for itself but also signifies a more abstract concept or idea	"Baby steps have a way of adding up to a lot of big steps."
tension	the feeling evoked by the conflicts of a fictional text	
theme	the main idea the writer wants to present. As the theme is usually not stated directly, the reader has to figure it out.	
tone	the tone the author uses to convey his/her attitude towards the subject	ironic, sarcastic, serious, sentimental, humorous
turning point	the point at which the action takes a different, often unexpected direction	

political speech	a formal address to an audience for political purposes, often to convince the listeners of the speaker's ideas	
alliteration	emphasis that occurs through the repetition of initial consonant letters of two or more neighbouring words	"bigger box", "red rose"
allusion	a reference to a familiar or famous historical or literary figure or event	"a King who took us to the mountaintop and pointed the way to the Promised Land" (Barack Obama refers to Martin Luther King, who explained his vision of America's future in his "I have a dream" speech.)
anaphora	the repetition of identical words or phrases at the beginning of a sentence or a line to put emphasis on sth.	"We'll establish free English courses. We'll establish new free Civics courses."
antithesis/ contrast	a contrast between two things; denotes the opposing of ideas by means of grammatically parallel arrangements of words, clauses or sentences so as to produce an effective contrast	"It used to be hot, it becomes cool. It used to be strong, it becomes weak." (Malcolm X)
antonym	→ *see poetry, p. 105*	
bias	→ *see cartoons/non-fictional texts, p. 108*	
conclusion	→ *see non-fiction, p. 107*	
ellipsis	→ *see poetry, p. 106*	
enumeration	naming each one of a series or list of things	
euphemism	a word or expression that people use when they want to talk about something unpleasant or embarrassing without mentioning the thing itself. It is used to spare the reader's feelings.	"to kick the bucket", "to fall off one's perch", "to pop one's clogs" are euphemisms of 'to die'.
exaggeration	representing (sth.) as being larger, greater, better, or worse than it really is	"We've heard this complaint a thousand times."

literary terms	definition	example
group of three	a group of three related ideas or concepts	"our openness, our hospitality and our belief"
introduction	the part at the beginning of any text	
inversion	the reversal of the normal order of words	"No longer can we believe in the truth of his words."
irony	a literary style employing contrasts for humorous or rhetorical effect	"In fact, it was his last big joke before his sense of humour calcified and had to be removed."
litotes	understatement, making sth./so. less important than in reality	"She's not as young as she was." = She's old.
metaphor	two ideas that are normally not linked are compared in a metaphor without using "as" or "like". This creates an image in the reader's mind and makes the description more powerful.	"They blazed a trail toward freedom through the darkest of nights." (Barack Obama)
paradox	a statement consisting of two parts that seem to mean the opposite of each other	"I can resist anything but temptation." (Oscar Wilde)
parallelism	the repetition of sentence pattern often used to contrast	"pay any price, bear any burden, support any friend"
point of view	the relation in which the narrator stands to the story, a mental viewpoint or attitude	
receiver-including words or pronouns	directly addressing the audience to create a sense of unity or identity	"we", "my friends", "fellow countrymen"
register	the level of language (degree of formality)	formal, informal, slang, …
repetition	repeating certain words or phrases for the purpose of emphasis	"different people, different beliefs, different yearnings, different hopes, different dreams" (Jimmy Carter)
rhetorical question	a question which expects no answer	"Don't we all want to become rich and famous?"
simile	→ *see short story, p. 105*	
symbol	→ *see short story, p. 105*	
theme	the main idea the writer wants to present. As the theme is usually not stated directly, the reader has to figure it out.	
tone	→ *see poetry, p. 107*	

drama	a work in prose or verse presenting a story which normally deals with a human conflict. It is usually intended to be acted on a stage as a play.	
act	one of the parts that a play is divided into. Each act is divided into two or more scenes.	Act I, scene II
acting time	the time the action of a narrative lasts as opposed to reading time	
action	everything that happens in a fictional text; events that form part of a play or film	In this scene, the action takes place in …

literary terms	definition	example
actor/actress	the person who performs in a play or film	
antagonist	the main character in opposition to the protagonist of a novel	
anti-hero	a main character in a novel or drama who does not have the qualities that a hero usually has, such as idealism or being morally good	
atmosphere	→ *see short story, p. 103*	
cast	noun: all the performers in a play or film verb: to choose an actor for a role in a play or film	
catastrophe	the unfortunate end of a story	
character	a person who takes part in the action of a fictional text	
characterization	→ *see novel, p. 114*	
climax/crisis	the most exciting or important moment in a story, event, or situation, usually near the end. This moment determines whether the situation will improve or grow worse. *Crisis* refers to the highest point of reader interest.	
comic relief	a humorous scene or incident in a serious play that relieves the tension	
conflict	the disagreement between opposing forces which is the basis of the plot of a play	
dénouement	the last part of a short story, book, play, etc. in which everything is settled	
dialogue	the words that characters speak in a fictional text, play or film	
dynamic character	→ *see novel, p. 114*	
exposition	the first part in a fictional text that provides background information and introduces the setting, the conflict and often the main character or character(s)	
falling action	the part of a story or play following the crisis/climax and leading to the dénouement or catastrophe	
flat character	→ *see novel, p. 114*	
foreshadowing	the technique of hinting at future events in such a way that the reader/viewer is prepared for them or can even anticipate them	
hero/heroine	the main character, protagonist, who usually has good qualities	
irony	a literary style employing contrasts for humorous or rhetorical effect	"In fact, it was his last big joke before his sense of humour calcified and had to be removed."
litotes	→ *see political speech, p. 117*	

literary terms	definition	example
mood	the feeling that the writer tries to evoke, such as excitement, anger, sadness, happiness, pity, etc.	
pace	the speed at which sth. happens or is done	
plot	a series of related events that make up the main story in a book, film etc.	
protagonist	the main character in a fictional text	
register	the level of language (degree of formality)	formal, informal, slang, …
rising action	the part of a fictional text following the exposition and leading to the climax/turning point	
round character	→ *see novel, p. 115*	
scene	a part of an act in a play or film in which events happen in the same place or period of time	
script (screenplay)	a written description of the dialogue and action of a play or film, including basic camera directions	
setting	the place and time at which the action of a fictional text takes place	
short plays and playlets	short in length, have few characters and usually deal with a single problem, conflict or event, which occurs in a single setting	
special effect	an unusual image or sound that has been produced artificially	
stage directions	notes in a play telling the actors how to speak and act. They also say what the characters and the stage should look like and where and when the action takes place.	"De Clerk's mobile rings." "Tom moves over to de Clerk and massages his shoulders and neck."
static character	→ *see novel, p. 115*	
structure	the organisation of the elements of a text	
subtext	the hidden meaning in a conversation, not expressed by words, but by intonation, tone of voice, facial expression, gesture, posture	
suspense	a feeling of excitement or worry that makes a reader curious about the outcome of a fictional text	
symbol	→ *see short story, p. 105*	
tension	the feeling evoked by the conflicts of a fictional text	
tone	→ *see poetry, p. 107*	
turning point	the point at which the action takes a different, often unexpected direction	

Glossary – alphabetical

	literary terms	definition	example
A	acoustic effects	effects relating to sound, e.g. in a play or a film	
	act	one of the parts that a play is divided into. Each act is divided into two or more scenes.	Act I, scene II
	acting time	the time the action of a narrative lasts as opposed to reading time	
	action	everything that happens in a fictional text; events that form part of a play or film	In this scene, the action takes place in …
	actor/actress	the person who performs in a play or film	Jesse Eisenberg as Mark Zuckerberg in "The social network"
	alliteration	emphasis that occurs through the repetition of initial consonant letters of two or more neighbouring words	"bigger box", "red rose"
	allusion	a reference to a familiar or famous historical or literary figure or event	"a King who took us to the mountaintop and pointed the way to the Promised Land" (Barack Obama refers to Martin Luther King, who explained his vision of America's future in his "I have a dream" speech.)
	anaphora	the repetition of identical words or phrases at the beginning of a sentence or a line	"Nobody hurt you. Nobody turned off the light … Nobody locked the door."
	antithesis/ contrast	a contrast between two things; denotes the opposing of ideas by means of grammatically parallel arrangements of words, clauses or sentences so as to produce an effective contrast	"It used to be hot, it becomes cool. It used to be strong, it becomes weak." (Malcolm X)
	antonym	a word that means the opposite of another word	night – day, wet – dry, hot – cold
	atmosphere	the feeling or mood created by the author through the description of events, setting, situation, etc.	"For a moment, a cloud drifted past the moon and the sky turned greenish gray."
B	bias	a prejudice in favour of or against one thing, person or group. It is a tendency to hold a certain point of view at the expense of other alternatives. An article is biased if information is presented in a one-sided way based on personal opinion rather than facts.	
	blank verse	a type of poetry without a rhyme, but with a regular metre. Usually a line has five unstressed syllables.	"To be, or not to be: that is the question: Whether 'tis nobler in the mind to suffer The slings and arrows of outrageous fortune,"
C	camera range	the distance between the camera and the object filmed	
	cameraman	so. who operates a camera for making films or TV programmes	

literary terms	definition	example
caption	words printed near or on a picture that explain sth. about the picture; a joke that is printed underneath a humorous drawing or photograph	
caricature	a presentation in which so.'s/sth.'s features are exaggerated to produce a comic or grotesque effect	
cast	noun: all the performers in a play or film verb: to choose an actor for a role in a play or film	
character	a person who takes part in the action of a fictional text	Grace in Dallas Woodburn's "Red"
characterization	The way in which a writer creates characters in a book, play, film etc. The author may present his characters in two ways: directly by describing them (explicit), or indirectly through their actions, thoughts or feelings and words (implicit)	"She has yellow hair, wiry legs, the most beautiful crooked smile in the world." "I was too lazy at school." "Audrey always sits opposite me, no matter where we play." → She seems to be interested
climax/crisis	the most exciting or important moment in a story, event, or situation, usually near the end. This moment determines whether the situation will improve or grow worse. *Crisis* refers to the highest point of reader interest.	
close-up	a full-screen shot of a person's face to show emotions revealed by their facial expression; it can also be used to draw attention to an object that is of particular interest to the plot or has a symbolic function.	
conclusion	the final part of a speech, an article or a piece of writing	
conflict	the disagreement between opposing forces which is the basis of the plot of a story or a play	
content	the kind of information a text contains	
crane shot	the camera is placed on a crane and moves in all directions. A crane is generally used for high angle shots.	
cross-cutting (parallel action)	combining shots of two or more scenes which are usually taking place at the same time	
D cut	a quick move from one shot to the next in a film	
dénouement	the last part of a short story, book, play, etc. in which everything is settled	
dialogue	the words that characters speak in a fictional text, play or film	
director (filmmaker)	so. who is in charge of making a film, or getting a play ready for performance, instructs the actors and the crew	David Fincher "The social network")
drama	a work in prose or verse presenting a story which normally deals with a human conflict. It is usually intended to be acted on a stage as a play.	

literary terms	definition	example
dynamic character	a complex character who may change (= round character)	Ed Kennedy in Markus Zusak's "I am the messenger"
E editing (montage)	the arrangement of shots in a structured sequence	
ellipsis	leaving out words to avoid repetition	"Anyone's guess."
end-stopped line	the end of a line	
enjambement	one line of poetry continuing to the next	
establishing shot	gives an overall impression of the location at the beginning of a scene	
euphemism	a word or expression that people use when they want to talk about something unpleasant or embarrassing without mentioning the thing itself. It is used to spare the reader's feelings.	"to kick the bucket", "to fall off one's perch", "to pop one's clogs" are euphemisms of 'to die'.
exaggeration	representing (sth.) as being larger, greater, better, or worse than it really is	"We've heard this complaint a thousand times."
explicit characterization	direct characterization by the narrator (telling). The author tells the reader explicitly about the character's looks, traits, attitudes.	"She has yellow hair, wiry legs, the most beautiful crooked smile in the world." "I was too lazy at school."
exposition	the first part in a fictional text that provides background information and introduces the setting, the conflict and often the main character or character(s)	
external action	the writer describes what the characters do	"Grace watched the pool of Vixen Red soak through the layers of paper towels." "Tears spilled from her eyes and *drip … drip … dripped* down her cheeks, …"
extreme close-up (detail shot)	shows an object in detail, emphasizing its importance in the scene	
eye-level shot	the camera looks straight at the person: this may suggest a neutral view, however, it can also mean that two people who are not on the same level for some reason (e.g. wealth, age, academic standing, social class) are presented as equal to each other.	
F fade-in	if a sound or picture fades in, it gradually becomes louder or clearer	
fade-out	if a sound or picture fades out, it gradually disappears	
falling action	the part of a story or play following the crisis/climax and leading to the dénouement or catastrophe	
fiction	a piece of writing that comes from a writer's imagination. Fiction is not factual but may be sometimes based on facts, real experiences or people the writer has known.	

literary terms	definition	example
field size (camera range)	the distance between the camera and the object filmed	
film	a series of moving pictures with sound that you can watch at the cinema or on television.	
flashback	a scene that shows what happened in the past and thus interrupts the chronological order of the plot	
flashforward	a scene that shows what may happen in the future and thus interrupts the chronological order of the plot	
flat character	a character who does not develop in the course of the action and is often a stereotype (= static character)	Ritchie in Markus Zusak's "I am the messenger"
focal point	the central point in a cartoon which is of interest	
foot	a unit of poetic metre consisting of stressed and unstressed syllables in any of various set combinations. For example, an iambic foot has an unstressed followed by a stressed syllable.	iamb: ˘ / → above trochee: / ˘ → standard
foreshadowing	the technique of hinting at future events in such a way that the reader/viewer is prepared for them or can even anticipate them	
free verse	a poem without a fixed metre or rhyme	
full shot	gives a view of the entire figure of a person to show action or to give an impression of a constellation of characters	
G genre	a particular style used in cinema or writing which can be recognized by certain features, such as subject matter, theme, type of characters, etc	novel, poem, short story, drama
group of three	a group of three related ideas or concepts	"our openness, our hospitality and our belief"
H heading	a title at the top of a page or a piece of writing	
headline	the title of a cartoon, a newspaper story, etc.	
hero/heroine	the main character, protagonist, who usually has good qualities	Ed Kennedy in Markus Zusak's "I am the messenger"
high angle shot	the camera looks down on the object so that it seems smaller, less important or inferior	
I iamb	a unit of poetic metre consisting of an unstressed followed by a stressed syllable	iamb: ˘ / above, today
implicit characterization	indirect characterization through action, behaviour, words, feelings and thoughts (showing). You learn a lot about a character by studying what he says and does, how he behaves in certain situations and interacts with others.	"Audrey always sits opposite me, no matter where we play." → She seems to be interested.
internal action	the writer shows the thoughts and feelings of the characters	"… but Grace felt a smile cracking her face."
introduction	the part at the beginning of any text (exposition)	
inversion	the reversal of the normal order of words	"No longer can we believe in the truth of his words."

literary terms	definition	example
irony	a literary style employing contrasts for humorous or rhetorical effect	"In fact, it was his last big joke before his sense of humour calcified and had to be removed."
L lighting	refers to the illumination of a camera subject being filmed. The lighting may be natural or artificial, very bright (high-key lighting) or dark (low-key lighting).	
line	a unit of verse ending in a visual or typographic break and generally characterized by its length and meter: a line of iambic pentameter.	
litotes	understatement, making sth./so. less important than in reality	"She's not as young as she was." = She's old.
long shot	provides a view of the situation or setting from a distance	
low angle shot	the camera looks up at a person so that people seem more important, powerful or even intimidating as it shows them in a superior position	
M main part	the body/main part of a book or document, not including the introduction or the notes	
match cut	two scenes that are connected by visual or acoustic means, e.g. a door is closed in one scene and opened in the following scene in a different context, someone is crying at the end of the first and the beginning of the second scene	
medium long shot	shows a person or people in interaction with their surroundings	
medium shot	shows a person down to the waist, often used to present two people in conversation	
metaphor	two ideas that are normally not linked are compared in a metaphor without using "as" or "like". This creates an image in the reader's mind and makes the description more powerful.	"They blazed a trail toward freedom through the darkest of nights." (Barack Obama)
metre	the pattern of stressed and unstressed syllables. Free verse has no regular metre.	
mood	the feeling that the writer tries to evoke, such as excitement, anger, sadness, happiness, pity, etc	
N narrative	any writing that tells a story	
narrator	a fictitious person who tells the story in a novel or film	
non-fiction	texts that give facts about real events, things or people	
novel	a fairly long fictional prose narrative. Normally it has a plot which develops through the actions, speech, and thoughts of its characters.	
O omniscient narrator	a narrator knowing everything about the characters	
onomatopoeia	words that sound like their meanings	"Boom. Boom. Boom."

literary terms	definition	example
open ending	a structural element in fictional texts in which the conflict remains for the most part unresolved	
overhead shot (bird's eye view)	makes an object seem less important, or gives orientation	
over-the-shoulder shot	often used to present two people in conversation: you are looking straight at one person from behind the second person	
P pace	the speed at which sth. happens or is done	
pan (panning shot)	the camera moves horizontally, i.e. to the left or to the right as opposed to tilting	
paradox	a statement consisting of two parts that seem to mean the opposite of each other	"I can resist anything but temptation." (Oscar Wilde)
paragraph	a section of a piece of writing that begins on a new line and contains a group of several interrelated sentences	
parallelism	the repetition of sentence pattern often used to contrast	"… look at you. Look at us …"
partial rhyme	the use of words which do not quite rhyme for poetic effect	"Daddy don't leave. Turn around please."
personification	the presentation of ideas, objects or animals as persons to make them more interesting for the reader	"That carrot cake with the cream cheese icing is calling my name."
perspective	the point of view from which a story is presented. The story can be told by a first-person or by a third-person narrator. The narrator can be a character in or outside the story. The third-person narrator can be omniscient (knowing everything about the characters) or limited (perceiving and knowing the same things as one character, seeing through the eyes of one character).	
play	a play is literature written for the stage	
poetry	a literary piece of writing characterized by musical (such as rhythm and rhyme) and literary elements (such as metaphor or simile). Poems are divided into lines and often grouped into stanzas.	
point of view	the relation in which the narrator stands to the story, a mental viewpoint or attitude	
point-of-view shot	assumes the perspective of one of the characters so that we seem to look through his eyes	
political speech	a formal address to an audience for political purposes, often to convince the listeners of the speaker's ideas.	
protagonist	the main character in a fictional text	Grace in Dallas Woodburn's "Red"
R reading time	the time it takes a person to read the story (as opposed to acting time)	
receiver-including words or pronouns	directly addressing the audience to create a sense of unity or identity	"we", "my friends", "fellow countrymen"

literary terms	definition	example
register	the level of language (degree of formality)	formal, informal, slang, …
repetition	words or phrases that are used more than once in a text, catching the reader's attention	"She knew this though: she loved kites and she loved rainbows. And, above all, she loved her mother."
reverse-angle shot	a sequence of point-of-view shots in which the perspective changes from one speaker to the other	
review	a report in a newspaper or magazine in which a critic gives his views of a new film, novel, etc.	
rhetorical question	a question which expects no answer	"What does it matter now?"
rhyme	the repetition of sounds usually at the end of two or more lines	"You've lost your head if that's how easily you're led."
rhyme scheme	the pattern created by the repetition of sound at the end of lines	abab, abba, cdcd, etc.
rhythm	the pace or "movement" of a poem. The rhythm is determined by the metre and by the length of sentences.	
rising action	the part of a fictional text following the exposition and leading to the climax/turning point	
round character	a complex character who may change (= dynamic character)	Ed Kennedy in Markus Zusak's "I am the messenger"
S scene	a part of an act in a play or film in which events happen in the same place or period of time	
script (screenplay)	a written description of the dialogue and action of a play or film, including basic camera directions	
sequence	a series of scenes which belong together	
setting	the place and time at which the action of a fictional text takes place	
short story	a work of fiction which usually deals with one or two major characters and one major conflict. The elements of a short story are character, plot, setting and theme.	
shot	a length of film without break; the smallest structural unit of a film	
simile	a comparison of two ideas, often linked by "as" or "like"	"Like a magic kingdom that belonged only to Grace and her mother."
soundtrack	all the recorded sound of a film (dialogue, sound and sound effects)	
special effect	an unusual image or sound that has been produced artificially	
stage directions	notes in a play telling the actors how to speak and act. They also say what the characters and the stage should look like and where and when the action takes place.	"De Clerk's mobile rings." "Tom moves over to de Clerk and massages his shoulders and neck."

literary terms	definition	example
stanza	a section of a poem consisting of a group of lines	
static character	a character who does not develop in the course of the action and is often a stereotype (= flat character)	Ritchie in Markus Zusak's "I am the messenger"
still	a photograph taken from one of the scenes in a film	
storyboard	a series of pictures that the director of a film uses to plan the action that will be filmed	
straight-on angle	the camera looks straight at the person: this may suggest a neutral view, however, it can also mean that two people who are not on the same level for some reason (e.g. wealth, age, academic standing, social class) are presented as equal to each other.	
structure	the organisation of the elements of a text	
style	the special, often personal and individual way in which a writer expresses ideas depending on personal factors and the type of text he/she is writing	
sub-heading	the title of one section of a longer piece of writing	
sub-plot	a plot that is subordinate to the main plot of a literary work	
suspense	a feeling of excitement or worry that makes a reader curious about the outcome of a fictional text	
symbol	an image that does not only stand for itself but also signifies a more abstract concept or idea	"Baby steps have a way of adding up to a lot of big steps."
T tension	the feeling evoked by the conflicts of a fictional text	
theme	the main idea the writer wants to present. As the theme is usually not stated directly, the reader has to figure it out.	
tilt (tilting shot)	the camera moves vertically, i.e. upwards or downwards as opposed to panning	
tone	the tone the author uses to convey his/her attitude towards the subject	ironic, sarcastic, serious, sentimental, humorous
tracking shot	the camera follows a person or an object	
turning point	the point at which the action takes a different, often unexpected direction	
V verse	a section of a poem consisting of a group of lines	
Z zoom in/zoom out	a stationary camera seems to move closer to or further away from the object, hereby focussing on it or showing it in its surroundings	

Copyrights

Bildquellenverzeichnis

Umschlag: Getty Images, München/The Image Bank/Lucas Lenie Photo

S. 6: *(Gleichgeschlechtliches Paar mit Mutter:)* alamy images, Oxfordshire; *(Familie in Latzhosen und Patchwork-Familie:)* fotolia.com, New York

S. 8: fotolia.com, New York

S. 22: *(1.)* fotolia.com, New York; *(2.; 3.; 4.)* alamy images, Oxfordshire

S. 23: *(5.)* alamy images, Oxfordshire; *(6.; 7.)* fotolia.com, New York: *(8.)* pixelio.de, München

S. 28: Cover zu Simon Hoggart und Emily Monk: "Don't tell Mum"

S. 29: D.C. Thomson & Co., Dundee, Scotland

S. 30: Sean Smith, Guardian News & Media Limited

S. 35: Mike Buscher, USA

S. 38: CartoonStock Ltd, Somerset, UK

S. 40: Off the Bone, Meiklejohn Graphics, UK

S. 41: *(1.; 3.)* CartoonStock Ltd, Somerset, UK; *(2.)* Copyright 2003 Tim Whyatt; *(4.)* off the mark.com, Melrose, USA

S. 45: CartoonStock Ltd, Somerset, UK

S. 47: from TIME magazine, (27.12.2010) © TIME magazine. All rights reserved.

S. 50: *(1.; 6.)* alamy images, Oxfordshire; *(2.; 7.)* Picture Press, Hamburg; *(3.; 5.; 8.)* Cinetext, Frankfurt/Main; *(4.)* Picture-Alliance, Frankfurt/Main

S. 56–57: *(1.)* akg-images, Berlin; *(2.)* Harald Thumser, Frankfurt/Main; *(3.; 4.; 6.; 7.; 9.)* Picture-Alliance, Frankfurt/Main; *(5.)* Bildagentur Huber/dpa; *(8.)* dpa-Zentralbild; *(10.)* alamy images, Oxfordshire

S. 58: Cover zu Mark Zusak: "I am the messenger"

S. 64: Cover zu Bali Rai: "(Un)arranged Marriage"

S. 67: *(Malcolm X und Martin Luther King:)* Picture-Alliance, Frankfurt/Main; *(Barack Obama:)* Shutterstock Images, New York

S. 68: alamy images, Oxfordshire

S. 69: Wikipedia

S. 72: Picture-Alliance, Frankfurt/Main

S. 92: CartoonStock Ltd, Somerset, UK

Textquellenverzeichnis

S. 8–10: "Red" © Dallas Woodburn, in *3 A.M.: A Collection of Short Stories*, iUniverse, USA, 2005, S. 81–86.

S. 17–21: "Ashes" © Susan Beth Pfeffer, in *Places I never meant to be: Original stories by censored writers*, Aladdin Paperbacks: New York, 1999, S. 114–125.

S. 24: "We remember your childhood well" © Carol Anne Duffy.

S. 27: "My Childhood" © Jahanvi, India, 2009.

S. 27: "My Father Thought It …" © Simon Armitage.

S. 28–29: three emails from "Don't tell Mum" © Simon Hoggart and Emily Monk, The Random House, UK, 2007.

S. 30–31: from "Gap years: Wasted youth?" by Patrick Kingsley, in *The Guardian*, 6 September, 2010, © Guardian News & Media Ltd 2010.

S. 35–37: from "Gap year before college gives grads valuable life experience" © G. Jeffrey MacDonald, 18.06.2008.

S. 38–39: from "Amy" © Mary Hooper, Bloomsbury: New York and London, 2002.

S. 39: from "Fever of the Bone" © Val McDermid, HarperCollins Publishers: New York, 2009.

S. 42–43: "NJ student's suicide illustrates Internet dangers" by Geoff Mulvihill und Samantha Henry, in *The Washington Post*, 01.10.2010. The Associated Press Copyright © 2010. All rights reserved.

S. 44–45: "How dangerous is the Internet for children?" by David Pogue, from *The New York Times*, (28.02.2008) © The New York Times. All rights reserved. Used by permission and protected by the Copyright Laws oft the United States. The printing, copying, redistribution, or retransmission of this Content without express written permission is prohibited.

S. 47: from "Will Facebook conquer the world?" by Shane Richmond and Will Heaven, in *The Telegraph*, 04.01.2011. © Telegraph Media Group Limited 2011.

S. 54: from "Hot or not? Website briefly judges looks" © Bari M. Schwartz, 04.11.2003.

S. 55: from "Person of the year 2010: Facebook's Mark Zuckerberg" by Lev Grossmann, in *TIME magazine*, (27.12.2010) © TIME magazine. All rights reserved.

S. 58–59: from "I am the Messenger" © Markus Zusak, published by Alfred A. Knopf, Borzoi Books, The Random House Group Ltd, New York, 2002. S. 14–21.

S. 64–65: from "(Un)arranged Marriage" © Bali Rai, published by Corgi. Reprinted by permission of The Random House Group Ltd, London, 2001. S. 15–18.

S. 67: Martin Luther King © 1963 Dr. Martin Luther King Jr; copyright renewed 1991 Coretta Scott King.

S. 68: "Party political speech" 1959 © Peter Sellers.

S. 69–70: Peter Debnam: "Australia Day Speech: Happy Australia Day!", Australia, 26.01.2007. © 2007 Peter Debnam.

S. 72–73: "I have a plan to destroy America", © 2004 Richard D. Lamm.

S. 74: from "Citizenship" by Mark Ravenhill, in *Shell connections 2005: New plays for young people*, faber & faber: London, 2005, S. 219–220. © Mark Ravenhill, Citizenship and Methuen Drama, an imprint of Bloomsbury Publishing Plc.

S. 76–78: from "A Vampire Story" © Moira Buffini, in *New connections 2008: Plays for young people*, faber & faber: London, 2008, S. 478–483.

S. 80–81: from "Citizenship" by Mark Ravenhill, in *Shell connections 2005: New plays for young people*, faber & faber: London, 2005, S. 230–233. © Mark Ravenhill, Citizenship and Methuen Drama, an imprint of Bloomsbury Publishing Plc.